SUCCESS
101

Other Books By Scott F. Paradis:

*Warriors, Diplomats, Heroes, Why America's
Army Succeeds*
Lessons For Business And Life

Promise And Potential
A Life Of Wisdom, Courage, Strength, And Will

And Coming Soon:

The Money-Go-Round
Get In On It!

SUCCESS
101

HOW LIFE WORKS

KNOW THE RULES, PLAY TO WIN

SCOTT F. PARADIS

Success 101: How Life Works -
Know the Rules, Play to Win

Copyright © 2012 Scott F. Paradis

Published and distributed by:

CORNERSTONE
ACHIEVEMENTS

Cornerstone Achievements
Post Office Box 256
Mount Vernon, Virginia 22121
www.cornerstone-achievements.com

ISBN: 978-0-9798638-4-4 (print, soft cover)

ISBN: 978-0-9798638-5-1 (e-book)

ISBN: 978-0-9798638-6-8 (print, hard cover)

Library of Congress Control Number (LCCN): 2012908074

Printed in the United States of America

We all yearn for connection and validation,
yet the truth is:

only when we love unconditionally
and share selflessly,

can we laugh freely, create magnificently,
and live fully.

Only then do we fulfill our purpose
for being in this world.

This book is dedicated to those ambitious and brave individuals, who when facing problems continue to search for solutions; when encountering obstacles continue to advance faithfully; and when confronting adversity continue to grow. For these men and women know that through their struggle life is made richer and fuller for us all.

CONTENTS

FOREWORD

You indeed are a success. You have breathed, you have moved, you have lived. The things you've seen, the places you've been, and the experiences you have embraced are unique to you. No one will ever travel your path in exactly the same way.

You have contributed a chapter to the grand epic. You have played a note for the resounding symphony reverberating through eternity. You have sung a moving verse in the majestic chorus. You have woven a seamless panel into the intricate tapestry of creation. Your life has been so much, and yet there is still so much more to come.

You possess talents and energy and a perspective needed in this world, needed by this world - needed more than you know.

All of heaven and earth - all people, all creatures, all things - await your gift, await your giving. You are here, in a time and place of your choosing, to add to life. Offer freely what you have - for as you do, another dream is fulfilled, another possibility is made real.

As for yourself, by giving you receive - in unimaginable measure. By sharing your life and your love you create your own reward: a prize for having taken the risk, for having ventured forth on this earth, for being and becoming.

To win at the game of life - to succeed, to live fully - you must play by the rules. There are just a few rules, but they are exceedingly important. Once you know the rules you can refine your skills and play to win. The task is not to get there first. It's not to claim the most. It's not to beat other people. You aren't competing with anyone. But everyone rejoices in your victory.

Success 101, How Life Works is a tome for realizing the fullness of life. You will find in these pages the insights of wisdom literature, success guides, and spiritual masters. You will find what you need to succeed and succeed wildly. *Success 101, How Life Works* is intended to help you realize: the search is over - the secrets are revealed. All you require is accessible to you.

You can have more life. You need only change your mind and adjust your course.

Your investment considering the words etched on these pages is an occasion you dissolve the gap between us, a gap in time and space - we journey as one. Join me on this journey of discovery, a journey of transformation. Our lives were never intended to be separate. We explore, we struggle, we succeed together. Your success is our success.

You are guaranteed to succeed!

Discover how life works...

1

WHAT IS SUCCESS?

Success is something we all desire. We all want to feel a sense of accomplishment, security, well-being. We all want to feel good and be happy. We know it is possible. We have felt the emotions of triumph, the delight of genuinely connecting with another person, the joy of achieving something worthwhile. We yearn to hold on to those feelings.

We see other people accomplish monumental tasks. They overcome nearly impossible obstacles, set world records, sustain loving relationships. They build huge organizations and serve untold masses. They influence the course of history.

We ourselves have tasted the fruits of success - the feeling of joy - if even only for an instant. We see people succeeding all around us.

Each one of us asks ourselves the question, Why can't I be more successful?

Is it a matter of nature?

Is it luck, fate, chance, that sets the doers, the achievers, apart from the sheep and the also-rans?

Should I have been born into the right family - one with status and wealth, with resources and means?

Is it my genes? Do I lack strength, endurance, speed?

Is it looks and demeanor that make the difference? Do I need a beautiful physique and a striking image?

How about brains? What if I'm shackled with an average IQ?

If only I could learn more quickly and know more. Maybe there aren't any opportunities left. Everything worth doing has been done. Timing is everything. Was I born at the wrong time, in the wrong place?

I don't have the social graces to win friends and influence people. Some people naturally are liked and popular. I'm not one of them. I'm not a natural leader. I couldn't get anyone to follow me out of a burning building. How could I ever succeed?

When we entertain doubt, these are questions that our minds struggle with. While your self-image may be lacking, and your sights may be set low, know this: success is not a matter of nature, or family, race or religion, status, or birth order. It doesn't matter what genes you inherited or what environment you find yourself in now. You are meant to succeed.

You are a success machine. You are intended to succeed. You possess all the skills, attributes, resources, and means to prosper. And not just to squeak by, but to succeed wildly. You have within you the ability to rise to great heights, to beat seemingly overwhelming odds, to contribute uniquely and spectacularly to the adventure of life. You are limited only by your conditioning and by the beliefs you claim as your own. Resolve, in this moment, here and now, not to allow yourself to fall victim ever again to challenging circumstances and negative attitudes. You have the power to achieve whatever you desire.

It is time for you to change direction - to head down a new path - to move from distraction to focus, from mediocrity to excellence, from despair to hope.

If you are a searcher and have been at your quest for any length of time, you have encountered a multitude of "secrets to success." There are literally thousands of messages and millions of messengers around you today. You have unlimited, nearly unfettered access to timeless truths and ageless wisdom. The "secrets" are captured in books and articles, writings and paintings, films and stories - they are concealed in literature, art, and architecture. Nature itself, the world around you, reveals the secrets daily. You just need to know where to look and be disposed to embrace the truth you encounter.

You can find the truth in religious traditions, in prayers and mediation. The secrets of success are literally being shouted from mountaintops. They are disclosed in the words you hear, the kaleidoscope of colors you see, the blend of impulses you feel. Sort through the noise and the chatter - listen - then move in the right direction.

The truth - the secrets - call out to you every day, over and over again. You can be so much more. You can experience so much more. You can become so much more. Do you really want to?

Upon intention, desire, and motivation, rests the story of your life. Your future - fears, tears, glory, and triumph - hang in the balance. What is it you want to do, experience, contribute, become?

If you are seeking a life of mediocrity, compromise, settling; if you would rather get by than get ahead; if you are willing to accept what comes your way rather than decide which way you will go - the choice is moot. This manuscript has nothing for you. An average, unremarkable, ordinary life is already your reality - you prove it, you live it, you reinforce it every day. Your decision is made.

But...

If the spark of yearning, of thirst, of hope, of desire still flickers, you have an opportunity to start life anew. No message or messenger can overcome a lack of ambition. However, if you are willing to learn, to act and to grow, you can alter the course and destiny of your life. You can embark on an extraordinary adventure. You can make what you have better, or you can start over and create something entirely new. It is up to you.

Now, I must provide you fair warning. Success is not for the faint of heart. Success in life rests at the cusp of courage, freedom, and responsibility. You are more powerful than you know. You must be willing to accept and wield that power and live with the consequences.

If grand ambition is not your style, at least keep your mind open to the possibility that "it is not written." The course you are on - that path you believe is a dead end - the road leading only to fear, and pain, and conformity - is not your only option. As long as you are breathing, you possess the ultimate power. You have a choice.

This manuscript brings together a multitude of perspectives. *Success 101, How Life Works* assembles ancient wisdom and contemporary insights. If you are open to it, the words you discover will speak to your soul, enlighten your mind, and energize your body.

While not every word will resonate with you, revealed in these pages is a communiqué, a message, you need to connect with. The truth is from a source ever so close to you. You will find the answers you seek and guidance to move in a new direction.

This is how life works.

THE SUCCESS SPECTRUM

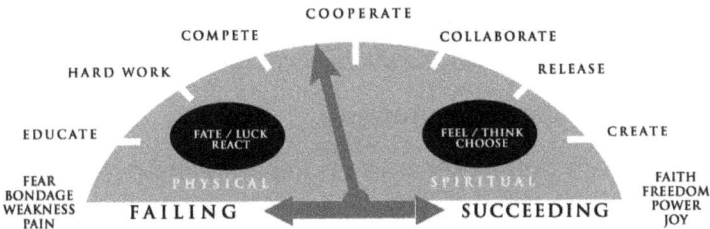

COOPERATE

COMPETE   COLLABORATE

HARD WORK   RELEASE

EDUCATE   FATE / LUCK   FEEL / THINK   CREATE
                REACT   CHOOSE

FEAR   FAITH
BONDAGE   PHYSICAL   SPIRITUAL   FREEDOM
WEAKNESS   FAILING   SUCCEEDING   POWER
PAIN   JOY

THE SUCCESS SPECTRUM

This illustration is meant to help you sort out in your mind distinctions evident in this dualistic reality - a world comprised of opposing forces, of opposites. Though not wholly adequate the Success Spectrum attempts to illustrate both direction and speed. Where you are along this continuum determines what you experience. The key is to move in the right direction in a way that accelerates your progress. Doing the right things in the right way is success.

We often reduce options to either-or choices when we really experience conditions along a continuum. You are on a path always moving toward something and away from something, but it rarely feels as though the choice is all or nothing. There are many routes to every objective. Life expresses itself in varied and limitless ways. But some choices are better than others. The challenge is to make the best choices.

To succeed, to live a full and fulfilling life, you must move toward your highest good. When you do, you encounter peace and love and joy.

The Success Spectrum is a gauge, a guide, a pictorial to help you discern where you are mentally. Thinking in a binary way (either or; moving toward something and away from something) you can use the diagram to assess your current disposition. Your predominant beliefs about life and how to succeed - how to get what you want - determine your course. Exploring and coming to understand what core beliefs you hold explains much about the circumstances you encounter, the trials you endure, and the success you enjoy.

What are you moving toward?

On one end of the spectrum is freedom and power and joy. On the other is bondage and fear and pain. Life offers degrees of these experiences everywhere in between. You get to choose.

The other component inherent in every motion is the speed of advance. Are you moving with energy and enthusiasm in a positive direction? Or are you feeling drained as you stumble toward some demise - conditions of weakness, of pain?

Life is comprised of opposing forces operating in multiple dimensions. You encounter these forces, engage these forces, respond to these forces. Instead of being a victim you can master these forces. You choose where you go and how fast you advance.

Ponder the Success Spectrum for a few minutes. Where do you place yourself on this spectrum?

Is the world physical and tangible? Or ethereal and spiritual? Is life subject to the whims of chance, fate, luck? Or is it governed by thoughts you think, feelings you feel, and choices you make? Is success the oft stated conventional wisdom: work hard, get a good education? Or does success require something more, something cooperative, a personal change?

To succeed do you need a positive mental attitude? Or will any attitude suffice? Do you need a competitive advantage? Or can you move beyond competition and collaborate? Is your life a chore, pure drudgery, a sentence you are serving? Or is it a creative adventure?

Is life a risk, a mystery, an unknown? Or can the truth be known, the way laid plain, the destination made real? Where are you on the scale of belief, of faith? You know you can do better.

You read these words with at least a tinge of hope in your heart. Without some modicum of desire you would not put forth the slightest effort. You need only reinforce that desire. The end state you seek is a way to advance, to progress, to grow, to succeed. Whether your sights are set on the stars or focused on ground beneath your feet - I ask you to make this journey with me. For...

> *Maybe I'll never be a billionaire, maybe I'll never be a sought after lover, or a sports superstar, or an international celebrity. Maybe I'll never become a political leader, or a musical genius, or a bona fide hero. I won't conquer or triumph, or amass immense wealth. I may never display any discernible talent. At the end of my days, I'll fade away into obscurity. My mark will be that I experienced the opportunity, I breathed the air, I absorbed the warmth of the sun, I felt the hope of each new day. I trusted in the promise. Though I may not have embraced my full potential, I took a chance, I made a leap. I got to feel life. No monument will ever be dedicated to my achievements, no parade or holiday will ever be devoted to my memory. Yet, despite it all, I did a small part. I journeyed here. In my imperfect way, I lived, I loved, I yearned to express more life. For in being alive, I succeeded.*

You are alive. You are guaranteed to succeed. You breathe the air. You yearn for something. You feel. The definitive question in living life is: What do you want to feel? How much life do you want to experience? Do you want to "get by" or do you want to excel? Are you content tending to the sidelines, or do you want to be in the fray?

Discover the secrets of success, the truth about how life works, and live life more abundantly.

What you seek, seeks you. What you want, wants you.

Keep moving in the right direction. That thing, your dream, your destiny, your treasure, is waiting patiently for you to arrive. It is very close. You need only make a minor adjustment. Start changing direction now. Get moving.

WHAT IS SUCCESS?

The word "success" conjures images of a life different from what you are experiencing now, does it not?

What images does success conjure for you?

Wealth - a mansion; a beach house; vacation villas; luxury cars; yachts; airplanes; first-class travel to exotic locales?

Health - fit and trim; athletic; free of disease and capable of ensuring you stay that way?

Influence - a profitable, prosperous, growing business; positions of status and stature within your community on corporate boards or within your current company or organization; membership in exclusive clubs; money in the bank?

Relationships - a great marriage or romantic bond; intimacy; happiness; well-adjusted, independent and prosperous children; financially comfortable and stable relatives – parents or siblings; admiration of friends and colleagues?

Fame - by way of a unique talent or achievement?

Enlightenment - complete knowledge of your purpose; an unquestioned conviction you are on the right path?

Freedom - no worries over financial issues, and the ability to devote your time, energy and talents to what you love?

How do you define "success" for you?

In this material society, success often means "things." That is, we equate prosperity to having more - more stuff, property, possessions, relationships, prestige. The interesting point here is, "having more" is what life is about.

The irresistible force in every living thing desires to have more life. In our infinite universe there is no limit to life's expanse. Every person's entire experience of life is about creating, experiencing - feeling - more.

Success is many different things to different people.

Success is always more, but it is not necessarily more *stuff*. Success is the fullness of life.

Success is a feeling.

Success is your birthright, your potential, your destiny.

Every life is a life of promise. Every adventure is filled with potential. Success is recognizing that promise, fulfilling that potential.

Life presents you with a choice in every instant. You can choose more life or you can resist.

Choose the better feeling - choose more life.

Success need not be grandiose. Success need not be affluence in the form of money, or property, or possessions.

Success is simpler than that - closer than that - more powerful and all consuming than the trappings of the material world.

Sometimes success manifests in a smile or a nod or a fleeting gesture. Success is realizing a moment of joy in the mayhem of existence. Success is connecting despite the forces that seek to divide. Success is uncomplicated, effortless, and true.

Success is a feeling - a good feeling.

If you were at the end of your life, in your final days looking back, would you say you recognized the promise of this life?

Did you avail yourself of the opportunities?

Did you make the most of your circumstances?

Did you nurture your talents and fulfill the purpose to which you were called?

Did you feel joy every chance you got?

No matter how you feel at this moment, realize there is no utility in regret - the could-a, would-a, should-a are all behind you now. Your opportunity was always in the moment. Did you make the most of it?

Did you succeed?

Success does mean more - more life.

Success ultimately is a feeling - a feeling of joy.

Choose to live your life more abundantly and embrace those moments of joy.

IS THIS ALL THERE IS?

A searcher's ultimate question: "Is this it?"

Is this all there is? Is life a fleeting and repeating series of what you've seen, where you've been, and what you've done?

As you read these words you sense that something more exists - something more real, something more true, some greater whole.

Only once you accept the truth that there is something more can you move beyond isolation and embrace a new, fuller life.

By looking you find light in darkness, hope in despair, calm in the storm; the one missing piece to make the puzzle whole and complete.

What you want, long for, dream about, and seek is to have life and have it more abundantly.

You can know no greater gift than to have life abundantly. When you accept the promise of life and embrace the potential of your existence in this time, place, and circumstance you release the chains that bind you, usher in newfound freedom to create, and experience ultimate peace and joy.

Usually people accept, without question, the physical reality around them, the boundaries defined by earth, sea, and sky. Similarly they accept the body as real, as real as the things one senses in the environment. We accept the things surrounding us as a matter of course, without reservation, and often without consideration.

We can verify physical phenomena. We confirm, through our senses, the substance of this reality - the rules that matter and energy conform to. We consult with one another, collaborate on what we experience through our senses to ultimately agree on what "is." This occurs, this confirming, for people all over this planet. The people agree, so it must be so - or is it?

Consider, for a moment, very carefully, very profoundly, that the physical reality you know and experience is not all there is.

When the wind blows, though we see branches sway and hear leaves rustle, do we see the wind? We don't see the wind, only its effects. Does that mean the wind is not real?

When man believed the world was flat - was it? No. The belief the world was flat limited opportunities. People dared not venture out to sea beyond the horizon.

Fearing the unknown people cling to the known and limit themselves.

If someone, sometime, did not envision a possibility that others could not see, if someone did not first consider the idea of "something more," we would still be living a subsistence existence. Man could not fly and space travel would still be fantasy; as would the generation, distribution, and application of electricity; the internal combustion engine; the telephone; the television; the computer. All technological advances, and even the complexity of human society, began as ideas - ideas most people held as unachievable, unrealistic, undesirable - beyond belief.

In practical terms, the idea of "something beyond our senses exists" is not difficult to accept. Mankind has discovered and exploited ranges of energy beyond the reach of humans' physical senses.

We communicate around the globe, we look through objects using light, sound, and magnetic forces, and we power machinery using forces biology cannot detect. These are but glimpses of endless possibilities yet to unfold, yet to explore, yet to create.

Skeptics claim, as skeptics through the ages have asserted, that man has reached the limit of his advance. Skeptics cling to an understanding of what is, through what they acknowledge and experience. By clinging to this idea of "what is, must, and can only be defined through our senses," skeptics rationalize and limit the possibilities of life. Skeptics proclaim, "Senses are king, long live the king."

However, something beyond this reality exists. Throughout history, by some means, the impossible became possible. Through the combination of ideas and action, what *could be* has become what *is*.

In the past, opportunities existed for something more, in the same way that opportunities still exist today.

Something beyond what we "know" and what we experience in this physical reality exists. Each and every one of us has the potential for so much more. This is not all there is.

FIGURED IT OUT YET?

It has been said of our human endeavor, "We are born wet, naked, and hungry. Then things get worse."

At times we hear the lament, "Life is like a beautiful melody, only the lyrics are messed up."

Or you might relate to this characterization, "The great business of life is to be, to do, to do without, and to depart."

All in all, hardly an endorsement of an adventure - rather more like an indictment of a trial.

Well, what is the meaning of life?

What is your purpose for being?

Have you figured it out yet?

For some, life is brief in time; for others life is brief in exploits. For those doubly cursed life is brief in both. For a few daring souls however, life is a magnificent adventure - an opportunity to achieve, an opportunity to connect, an opportunity to be and become, to feel fulfilled.

If only we all could embrace the opportunities - to promote laughter instead of tears, encourage growth instead of stagnation, pursue fulfillment instead of comfort, bestow our treasure of priceless gifts and unique personal talents, and in return receive the inexhaustible support of other people sharing theirs.

The essence of the human endeavor - the way to good feelings - is to relate and to create.

The end product of relating and creating is joy. Through these pursuits we give of ourselves, we share our gifts. In giving we make a rightful attempt to achieve our mission in life.

Human beings are social creatures on a journey of discovery. We relate to this environment. We relate to other people. We relate to circumstances. All we encounter we process from the limitations of our physical ability to engage, our intellectual capacity to interpret, and our penchant to observe, and often judge, from a given perspective.

While you process all you encounter, seek to contribute to the weave - the tapestry of the enterprise - the grist of the tale.

Seek to leave a creative mark - a legacy to your having passed this way. Relate to what is and create what you come to believe can be. As all life is about feeling, leave good feelings in your wake. You will be loved for it.

Imagination is your guide to fashion something new out of existing circumstances. Through your prevailing thoughts you unearth and create the drama (comedy, tragedy, love story) you become party to. Relate and create as a matter of course and as the purpose for your being.

Distinguished another way: life is a quest - a mission - a mission revealed by living it. For some the mission is explicit and defined. For others the mission is imprecise and ill defined - ripe for interpretation. In attempting to complete your mission you might embark on off-road excursions and wander into uncharted territory. Life carries you both where you request to go and where you should go. If where you are feels good and feels right, you have chosen your path well. If what you encounter troubles you, choose again, and learn from your choice.

Relate to what is. By contributing to life you receive more life.

Creating is your donation. Relating to creation is your reward.

You have a note to sing to make the melody of life sweet. You have a chapter to write to complete the saga. Your time is not lost, nor your efforts advanced in vain. The purpose of life is as simple as this: relate to what you encounter and create what the world lacks. Love life and life will love you. If you do the part prescribed precisely for you, you will live a full and fulfilling life, relating and creating. You will feel joy.

The Cherokee expressed it another way:

> *"When you were born, you cried and the world rejoiced.*
>
> *Live your life so that when you die, the world cries and you rejoice."*

Understand that your purpose in life is to relate and to create. Through these actions, you feel.

Get busy. Opportunities are unlimited but your time is not.

Figured it out yet?

LIFE IS A JOURNEY

Your life is a journey, a passage through time. You perceive it as a voyage from one place and moment to the next, unfolding and forever in motion. Yet every journey begins from the same place and every journey has as its purpose the same end.

The place to begin is where you are now; the purpose is to achieve your destiny.

Is your life filled with questions?

Often those questions substitute for getting on with the task at hand - moving, acting, living. By posing questions and pursuing "new" answers you think you will find a reasoned way home, a way and a means that is direct, clear, and challenge-free.

You search and search because the answers you have do not satisfy ego - that part of yourself grounded in physical reality. Stop searching for answers, step out on your journey.

Here are the answers that matter:

You will achieve your destiny by acting on faith, by letting go of the things you cling to, and by forgiving those who have wronged you. Unimaginable joy awaits.

This reality is dynamic, constantly changing. You are immersed in creation, immersed in the journey of life. Ultimately, all is illusion. The gift of free will is key to the choice you must make, the option you must ultimately pursue.

Cry if you might, but through those tears refuse to be a pawn to your emotions. Use your emotions as the guides they are intended to be. Respect them, respond to them, and by so doing master them.

Become a brave pioneer - a sojourner for which comfort is not your calling, nor appeasement your way. Do not allow complaints and derision to serve as justification. Freedom and fulfillment come not on the easy road.

Realize freedom and fulfillment by overcoming fear and acting on faith.

The road to your destiny, the course you set, lies before you. Take the next small step and contribute something positive with the gift of your life.

The only recourse to advancing gloriously in life is to

retreat to a hovel of comfort - a vain and shallow harbor. From there you can worship idols of wealth and status at a safe distance, 'til bondage and death overcome.

Complete the simple, yet paradoxically difficult, task of life: let go of ego, dissolve the illusion. You have a will for this purpose - it's your desire to change.

You have a wellspring of strength from a source you cannot see but know is real. If you have the courage to proceed, one step at a time, you will surely arrive.

Before you are two well-defined choices: 1) Exercise your free will to suffer in the illusion; or 2) Journey to your destiny. You can either embrace ego and resist, compete, and survive in the illusion; or embrace truth and go with the flow, accept, create, and rejoice.

If you choose wisely, you ally with truth and forego a separate will, a separate "I." If you choose poorly, harden yourself for a lonely journey dominated by ego, flush with fear.

You have a sense your experience of life could be much more than it has been.

It can be!

What you think you lack you can in fact find. The place to start is where you are.

Look for the answers where the answers are found: within.

There is no other door, no other route to where you are supposed to go. Your life is a journey.

The world is in motion. Instead of flailing about, searching for an easy way, let go of fear and listen to the still small voice within. Go through the middle.

Act by faith and your life will steer to its destiny.

PERFECT IS NOT A POINT

Ah, but for the perfect moment, the perfect day, the perfect life.

With enough moments one makes a day, with enough days one makes a life.

Maybe perfection is not too much to strive for, not too much to hope for, not impossible to achieve.

Remember in high school geometry you learned that a perfect line or a circle, or any figure for that matter, can only exist in the abstract. In the real world, any representation of a geometric shape taken to its finest measure will reveal itself as imperfect, deficient in some way.

In a reality in constant motion, only for the briefest instant is every atom in perfect alignment - a rare occurrence indeed. But though the abstract versions of shapes do not exist, in practice, imperfect representations work quite well for the purposes to which people apply the concepts.

You see, in this life perfection is not a point. Perfection is a range.

What makes for a perfect experience?

The environment must be just so.

The weather just right. A more than comfortable temperature - not too hot, not too cold. Not too wet, not too dry. A fresh breeze perhaps.

The circumstances must be ideal.

The right person or people in the right frame of mind, with the right intentions; a complementary energy. A synergy of sorts.

And the activity must be idyllic; engaging, entertaining, challenging, inspiring perhaps.

The ingredients of an ultimate experience must come together in a union of time and place and people. When the ingredients converge in vital measure they achieve perfection - but never will a perfect moment repeat itself.

Perfection is not a point. Perfection is a range.

In the same way, success is not a destination; success is a journey.

People declare quite frequently the weather is perfect. One may consider the events of a day as being perfect. The judgment one renders is not for perfection in every instant, every color, every contrast, every image, word or deed. Rather the label one might affix to perfection is a product that on the whole renders one satisfied and fulfilled.

You might have imagined a life different from what you have experienced to this instant. Maybe you imagined yourself wealthier, healthier, fitter, more capable, more determined. Maybe you had hoped to have more possessions, more peak experiences, or to see more of the world. Maybe life was intended to be an unencumbered journey or maybe a trail to be traveled with a soul mate still to be found. Maybe you pictured yourself mastering some task, displaying a rare talent, leading an uncommon effort. Maybe in your mind's eye you imagined yourself more beautiful or more handsome, attractive, and appealing.

Well, none of these things need be a point to strive for. You see, perfection is not a point. Perfection is a range.

You entered life with a lockbox of possibility. Unlock the chest and lift the heavy lid and you will discover a treasure trove of adventure. You have time and talent. You have desire and abilities. You have a means to relate to others and to this world. You have the resources to realize heights you have never even imagined.

None of the individual components of your life need be perfect. The environment need not be pristine. The circumstances need not conform to some ideal. The people surrounding you need not be faultless. You need only find a synergy of intention and an enthusiasm of purpose.

One person declares a meal perfect, a work of art perfect. Another will disagree. One person's conception of perfection will not match another's. Any perfect encounter will never be the same as any other perfect encounter. The challenge to living perfect moments, leading to perfect days, leading to a perfect life, is realizing that you judge perfection. Judge less harshly.

Perfection exists in the abstract, but for you, in this world, in your time and space, accept that perfection is not a point; perfection is a range.

Expand your range that you might experience perfection more and more often until you build the perfect life. Nurture those seemingly insignificant good feelings until they become feelings of bliss. Then you will have succeeded.

BELIEVE IN LIFE

What do you believe in?

Do you believe in destiny?

Do you believe in the system?

Do you believe in yourself?

In life after death?

In God?

We typically think of the word "belief" as an opinion or conviction about something - an existence not immediately susceptible to rigorous proof. The truth, however, is that your beliefs shape what you experience in this reality. What you believe matters.

The origin of the word "belief" offers a telling verse.

Belief is a compound word with parts synonymous to: "be" - "by" and "lief" - "live." Taken together, the meaning of something we "believe in" is something we "live by."

This etymology sheds light on the age-old debate between the advocates of *faith* as a means to salvation and those who assert that *works* are key to a full and fulfilling life. The word "belief" means that acts and faith are inextricably linked. What you do, the actions you take, are in accordance with your beliefs.

The proof of your faith is in your works. The truth of your words is in your deeds.

Relying on this meaning of the word suggests that beliefs determine a worldview inextricably linked to how you live. Rational explanations (or intellectual fabrications) notwithstanding, beliefs organize your life. You do what you believe.

So, again: What do you really believe?

You can determine this only by observing how you live, how you respond to others, how you respond to the world around you, and what you in fact do. Honestly assess yourself. Do you like what you see? Is it time to change?

By nature we are a nostalgic breed. It may be the distance of time, but it seems the only thing people prefer to the way things *are* is the way things *were*. We seek security in the past and attempt to prolong the glory of prior triumphs. We resist change. But life doesn't work that way. You see, life is on the move, life is constant change.

You are on a journey from where you are to where you are meant to be. The key, the secret, is moving in the right direction. Instead of reminiscing or pining for the past, begin where you are now. Though you may temporarily succumb to doubt and fear, or mistakenly take a path of least resistance, recognize progress in this reality entails struggle and involves risk. It is time to act; it is time to change beliefs, to be what you really are, to become whole.

The purpose of life is to grow and expand - and in doing so, you *feel*.

Sometimes (you might say often) the prospects of growth, with their attendant trials and tribulations, are uncomfortable and at times painful. The thing about life is that you cannot get from the start to the end without going through the middle. So if you aspire to grow, if you aspire to learn, if you aspire to be and become - aspire to live.

Believe in life and you will act accordingly.

YOU HAVE ALL YOU NEED

Russell Conwell, the founder and first president of Temple University, told the story of "Acres of Diamonds" to illustrate just how often we misplace our focus:

A wealthy landowner, in central India, was living a full and contented life - until he learned of the magnificence and power of diamonds. The landowner, obsessed by the prospect of possessing such radiant jewels, concluded his life was not that full after all. He sold off his property, abandoned his family - in short, he risked everything, vainly seeking something he believed he lacked. Desperate and broke after years of searching, he cast himself into the sea. The tragedy of the tale is that after the man began his quest the new owner of his property discovered, in a stream the former landowner had often cooled himself beside, the richest deposit of diamonds in the world. That former landowner had literally walked away from acres of diamonds, ending his life in despair, because he did not know what treasure he possessed.

Is this a true story? You bet. It's a story that has been lived millions of times by millions of people. People willingly abandon their greatest assets in search of something they mistakenly believe they lack.

People search frantically for what they do not know - a place for themselves in this world, a place yet to find. Some people wallow in the despair of longing. Others ache with a sense of emptiness, craving something more. In response to the ache, many shackle themselves to the will of ego. In this desperate game, success, fulfillment, happiness are in distant lands, beyond the next river, over the next hill, always around the next elusive corner. Motivating the search are fortune, fame, love, security, power - attributes people believe they do not possess. The moral of "Acres of Diamonds" rings true still. We travelers - adventurers, ordinary people living ordinary lives - have what we need to succeed in this life.

You need not covet something elusive; you need only recognize and appreciate the treasure you possess - your acres of diamonds.

The distance from despair to fulfillment, from longing to abundance, from sorrow to celebration, is a realization in your mind. Recognize your acres of diamonds.

The story of every life, though at times perceived as a disparate trek, is actually an element of an intricately woven tapestry. You are not poor and dispossessed. You are not separate and alone. You have been awarded a great treasure. Weave your cord and add it to the grand tapestry. Fulfill the destiny that is your potential.

Do not despair in the game of hide and seek, searching unceasingly. What you are looking for is hidden in plain sight, surrounding you, protecting you, loving you, in spite of your foolishness.

Use the time, talent and energy you have, for these are your acres of diamonds.

Your task is to mine those acres of diamonds for a greater purpose.

You have all you need to live a full and fulfilling life. Use what you have.

Success is a good feeling - a feeling you choose.

2

THE SECRET OF SUCCESS

We dance round in a ring and suppose,

But the secret sits in the middle and knows.

- Robert Frost -

M y hope is that you are approaching this chapter
with great excitement and anticipation. For in
these next few pages you will discover the "secret of
success" - that indispensable principle, that unique element, that distinguishes a common, ordinary life from
an extraordinarily successful, full and fulfilling life.

If you adhere to the "secret" revealed in these pages
you will generate, produce, create a lifetime of positive
feelings. You will succeed. This is the way life works.

We - you and I - are not separated by time and space,
but rather we journey together on this noble quest. The
words you now read are timeless thought energy that
I leave here for you. Your enthusiasm, combined with
mine, releases (combines and redirects) new energy to
aid others who continue to seek.

Approach this phase of your expedition with the innocence of a child. Release any preconceptions. Enjoy
and embrace the moment. Soak in truth with eager ex-

pectancy. The act of connecting with and finally understanding, simply and completely, truths that are at once palpable and profound, is going to change your life.

As you conclude the last sentence in this chapter it is my intent that you understand and begin to internalize two simple, but weighty revelations:

1) The "Secret of Success" - that characteristic, the activity, separating "high achievers" from everyone else.

2) "Your Ultimate Power" - the means you apply to shape your life and times.

Upon grasping the two truths, consciously and seriously consider the implications and the potential they herald. Taking responsibility for your life, setting your course, and wielding the ultimate power will make a colossal difference as to the value, the integrity, and the richness of life - not just of your life, but the lives of all the souls who share the journey with you.

Claiming your power and focusing it, as the secret of success requires, will revitalize you. You will not be the same person.

You are about to discover something both incredible and wonderful. The secret is uniquely extraordinary and exceptionally potent. Don't dismiss or take these words lightly. Your ordinary journey is about to become extraordinary.

Rather than building to a great reveal, I'll express these truths, up front, now, as clearly and succinctly as possible.

As the implications of what you are about to discover are profound, the remainder of the chapter is intended to assist you in removing doubt and nurturing faith, so that you can understand and apply the power these statements make known.

The Secret of Success:

MOVE IN THE RIGHT DIRECTION.

Your Ultimate Power:

THOUGHT.

You were probably hoping for something more...

These truths seem at once unremarkable and self-evident. These features, being unremarkable and self-evident, are, however, characteristics of all profound truth.

The "secret" is comprised of two elements: the first demands action; the second, effort along a preferred or optimum course. The optimum course is the way of your highest potential; the full expression of your greatest gifts - it is the way to experience your supreme joy. You are meant to succeed.

Anyone and everyone who moves in the right direction will succeed. People moving in the right direction create, experience, and receive in a measure the poor lost souls - those individuals resisting any advance, or those heading in the wrong direction - are astonished to observe. Moving in the right direction is the key to living a full and fulfilling life.

When you move in the right direction, you are working with and harnessing the power of your thoughts. Moving in the right direction literally changes your life. Harmonizing with the purpose of life, you climb to new heights, hear with greater fidelity, see with exacting clarity, and feel with immense conviction. Life is more enjoyable, more enabling, more exciting.

Moving in the right direction you achieve unparalleled success and realize the objective Aristotle determined to be the purpose of life: **HAPPINESS!**

Moving in the right direction - applying the ultimate power of thought - has built fortunes and enabled righteous kings. It has established new civilizations and eradicated disease and suffering. It has brought people enduring love and profound peace. Understanding and following the mandate of moving in the right direction allows you to choose to amass a great fortune, achieve singular distinction in a given field, and find unconditional love.

The assertion, "Move in the right direction," elicits a straightforward and very legitimate question: How?

The clarification of "How?" leads us to the means of personal power: *thought.*

Thought guides the direction of every life. Thought is the one aspect of life the individual controls. Thought is the mechanism by which we choose. And by our choices we choose what will be.

Thought is also the gateway to ultimate power - to an all-knowing, everywhere present, all-powerful ultimate reality. Thought is the channel from the material world of sight and sound to the ethereal world of spirit and truth.

While all of life is experience, thought is the only thing we control. Our ultimate power resides in thought - what we think, what we focus on, what we call forth.

Your thoughts are your responsibility. Your thoughts determine your life.

Accepting full responsibility for your life and employing the ultimate power of thought moves you in the right direction. When you move in the right direction, your journey becomes a grand adventure, and each day is filled with pure delight.

If this revelation has not invoked a spark of excitement, more explanation is necessary.

Before you proceed, I offer a warning:

You have access to and possess an irresistible force. A force so powerful it has literally transformed lives and altered the course of human history. It is a force for good, for noble purposes, for progress, but it can be misapplied. You see that "force" always produces. It creates results, good or bad, surely, consistently, and continuously. And it can be misdirected.

The good news is that in the end, right always triumphs. Well-being always prevails. Life gets its way. Life intends to grow, and it shall.

Temporarily however, circumstances can appear negative. That force can generate more trial than triumph, more mayhem than majesty, more pain than pleasure. Even these temporary, negative conditions, however, serve a positive purpose. Even "negative" conditions offer opportunities for learning, opportunities for growth, opportunities to choose again.

The method (moving in the right direction) and the means of success (employing the power of thought) are both mysterious and unmistakably evident.

Your life vindicates the functioning of these principles. Your life is full and fulfilling when you move in the right direction. When you either refuse to move, or move in a direction other than the right one, your life presents lessons for growth and opportunities for change.

Your best choice is to choose to focus the energy of thought on moving in the right direction.

The ultimate power - the power beyond thought - the energy beyond existence - has been and always will be available to you wherever you are, whenever you need it. This force, you have access to and can control. Unfortunately most people shy away from its power and relegate themselves to a life of what could have been.

Unaware or afraid of the truth, people who fail to connect live lives that are but a shadow of all they can be.

Being able to express the method or means of success in words is neither a requirement for wielding the power of creation, nor for charting a progressive course. Countless people have succeeded wildly not because they understood intellectually the concept of success, but rather because they consciously or unconsciously availed themselves of means to employ their power.

Successful people knowingly or unwittingly move in the right direction - the direction that leads them to their highest good - to a full and fulfilling life - to joy, peace, love. This secret of success - move in the right direction - does not explain how life works; rather it instructs that somehow life works for those who move in the right direction.

THINKING A LITTLE HARDER

Let us here now circle back to prepare your mind to embrace these astounding revelations.

Consider these truths from a broader perspective. More than reading words, you have before you an opportunity to internalize timeless truth. Grasping the secret's simplicity and potential amazes and astonishes. Embolden your spirit to renew your life.

Having been exposed to the message, some fail to grasp the underlying meaning. This may elicit a less-than-positive reaction. If these truths did not ring clear for you, the excitement, the anticipation, and the eager hope with which we began likely dissipated like air sputtering from a punctured balloon.

If these two statements - "To succeed, move in the right direction" and "Your thoughts create your reality" - do not speak to you - if instead of an empowering revelation you feel you have unearthed disappointment - stick with me until the end. We will grow together.

If these statements ring hollow, or if you feel disillusioned and mistakenly believe you have stumbled upon another dead end in your long and fruitless search for success, think again. Prepare your mind to be fertile soil. The veil of secrecy may finally be lifted. With your vision clear and your spirit resolute you may embrace a new way - a new reality. The secrets are nothing less than the means to make your life full and fulfilling.

The words of the truth expressed in these pages have likely elicited one of three responses:

1) Validation - the words confirm what you, deep in your being, know to be true.

2) Disappointment - you, in error, believe you have, yet again, been duped.

3) Inadequacy - though you accept the wisdom, you struggle to understand how to apply the power to your humble, perplexing or troubled circumstances.

Taking a moment to prepare your mind will permit the best of all possible outcomes.

Steps to prepare your mind:

1. Accounting for the Limitation of Words (for interpretation and understanding).

2. Establishing a Common Perception (defining reality; learning the rules).

3. Setting Your Mind (releasing skepticism, resistance, fear).

Truth is unerring, ageless wisdom. Words however, don't always strike the right chord. So what follows is the truth expressed in a myriad of ways, all succinctly but tellingly. The way to success, the secret, is simple and clear. You need only accept the truth and make it your own.

The truth beckons, but the choice is yours. You can choose to accept or reject the power of the truth. If you embrace it, your life will change - maybe not all at once, but in a measure of time it will change dramatically. You will begin life afresh.

If, however, you reject the truth you will remain where you are - lost in a maze. Your search will continue. But, no worries, no regrets, do not fear; the truth, the path, the means to success is always at hand. The power the secret reveals follows you down every dark corridor; it waits patiently at every confusing intersection. The truth is an enduring friend.

ACCOUNTING FOR THE LIMITATION OF WORDS:

Language, particularly written language, for all its beauty, subtlety, and strength, fails the task of complete expression. Insightful ideas captured and reduced to words, however, still serve as useful tools to help us crawl, inch by inch, toward our inevitable destination.

Sometimes on rare, extraordinary occasions language strikes a chord of spirit and resonates a heretofore unfathomable truth in a simple, heartfelt way. When this happens our lives propel forward; life experience transforms.

Look beyond mere words for meaning.

> *Ignorant people are unable, even unto*
> *death, to abandon the idea*
> *that in the fingertip of words there is the*
> *meaning itself,*
> *and will not grasp ultimate reality*
> *because of their intent to cling to words.*

> - LANKAVATARA SUTRA -

Words are, in fact, twice removed from reality. Words are symbols attempting to express concepts. Concepts in turn are attempts to represent reality. Seek not merely the words and concepts, but the reality.

Words exist because of meaning;
once you've gotten the meaning,
you can forget the words.

- CHUANG TZU -

Philosophers and writers throughout the ages have lamented their attempts to reduce an idea, a concept or a thought to a brief, succinct, but complete expression. As Henry David Thoreau once proffered, "Excuse the length of my writing for it would require more time to be brief."

You can argue that I exhibit the same failing, but you cannot lay blame on the words of truth.

The work has been done, the time invested to condense and refine a simple but monumental truth to but a few powerful words. Embrace the truth.

ESTABLISHING A COMMON PERCEPTION:

At its most basic, "reality" consists of two elements: energy and awareness (more on this in the *How Life Works* chapter). What we experience is energy; that we experience is awareness. Our senses may not be able to discern what exists beyond our time and space, but exploring the component parts of reality will help us recognize truth.

Given two elements (energy and awareness), human beings deal with two constants: the observer and change. There is you and there is everything else. That is, you recognize or experience (observe) the continuous motion of energy (change).

You and everything else in this reality are on a journey. You are traveling from where you began to where you will end.

You are in the midst of a grand dance with the cosmos. You experience change in the rising and setting of the sun, in your movements doing commonplace things over the course of ordinary days; in your interactions with friends, coworkers and loved ones. Everything you stumble upon and interpret in this physical universe - people, places and things - is moving, changing, evolving. Nothing stays the same.

You are in the extraordinary position to observe remarkable happenings and actually feel the change.

You take in energy impressions all day everyday - 24/7. You are a receiver. You receive and interpret stimulus, stimulus from the environment, stimulus from other people, and stimulus that rises up from a source within. You experience - you feel - that stimulus.

You receive and interpret the dance of energy coming at you through your physical senses and through some undefined aspect of your being - something you may sense as surreal but in your heart know is very real. A force, an impulse, a feeling stirs within you. A still, small voice calls. Something guides you through a whisper or an urge. While this guide intends for you your highest good, the choice is always yours.

Most people, mistakenly, cast that aspect of themselves - the whisper; the still, small voice - aside. In a material world, where only the tangible seems to matter, disregarding the whisper, the still, small voice, causes people to lose their way. For your own good, cultivate a means to listen.

While change is a persistent component of reality, awareness too is self-evident. Without you observing there is nothing to observe. Awareness is consciousness. It is your privileged position to observe the cosmic ballet of the energy at play. More than an observer however, you are party to a splendid celebration, a universal gala, an iconic unveiling. You are immersed in a world of possibility. You feel your way through life. You are on a journey, rocketing forward on a multi-dimensional thrill ride.

Are you holding on for dear life? It's time you let go. Throw up your hands and embrace the sheer exhilaration of the ride.

This journey you are on - the game you have chosen to play - has some rules:

Your life is a paradox: You are both a bit player in a master production and the main event. The story is bigger than you, but the story is all about you.

Life has a purpose. Life's purpose is to expand and to grow. Your reason for being is to contribute to that purpose by feeling.

The boundaries are set.

> Every journey has a beginning and an end. You transitioned into this life, you will transition out. Your immediate task is to make the most of the opportunities before you.

> Your body must conform to the limitations of this reality. You are subject to gravity and all the other forces of nature. You are part of, and depend on, an environment (air, energy, nutrition) to survive. As a physical being you grow, mature, and age.

You are not alone. You are nurtured and challenged by a supporting cast. Your journey is a social venture, a collective quest. You help others, they help you.

You receive in proportion to what you give. There is no such thing as "something for nothing." All life directs, channels, manipulates energy to create something new. If you intend to experience something substantial you must put forth effort. You must give to get.

You are not separate from divine reality. Though you may ignore the truth, and believe you are lost and alone in a dangerous place, you are being guided and loved every step of the way. Though the illusion appears real, it is still but an illusion.

While you are aware, you are more than awareness and more than a receiver. You have a gift. You are powerful. You operate the ride. You are a creator.

Thoughts and feelings, your thoughts and feelings, are energy. Through thought and feeling you have the ability to interact with and manipulate energy, the environment, the very circumstances you experience. You alter your own reality. And through thought and feeling you have access to the ultimate power, a power beyond time and space.

The one thing you control in life is the universal remote. In your mind you change the channel. Your thoughts and feelings are your power, and allow you access to ultimate power.

SETTING YOUR MIND:

You are a creator.

The most powerful, most often overlooked and most misunderstood "rule of the game" is this:

Thoughts becomes things.

Your mind is the one asset over which you alone have absolute control. By means of thought you can and do adjust your feelings. Through your thoughts you fashion your reality. Through thought you create the life you experience.

You have intellect, you have emotion, you have a body - these are all tools to help you navigate, explore, and create in a material world. These are resources to assist you on your journey. Your primary tool, however - the one that influences your feelings - is thought.

Your key asset is thought.

You employ your thoughts and feelings often without consideration. You use the assets at your disposal to shape the feelings you feel, and in turn influence the environment you experience and the circumstances you encounter. Thoughts are a form of creative energy. That creative energy moves from mind to body. Creative energy manifests in the physical world.

Thought drives all the change you experience. Thought is working, forming, acting in whatever direction you choose. Even if you neglect or seek not to choose, the energy of thought is working on life. A mind running wild produces an uproar. Rather than let the creative force run rampant and uncontrolled, manage it and guide it.

If nothing else, choose to generate good feelings. Good feelings alone will take care of the rest.

CONTROL YOUR THOUGHTS.

As master of your mind, you are much more powerful than you now know. By disciplining thought you manage your power.

You possess power to the degree you assume responsibility for your quest and control and direct your thoughts. If you shun responsibility you forfeit power. You enjoy ultimate power only if and when you accept complete and total responsibility for your thoughts and therefore your life. For your life, your station, your accomplishments, your failings, are but the product of the thoughts to which you have given energy.

If you blame others or circumstances, or offer excuses; if you invent alibis for why you are not where you desire to be; if you claim you are too young or too old, too big or too small, too dumb or too smart, too ugly or too beautiful, too afraid, lost and alone to succeed; then your reasons form crutches for failure. Excuses only rationalize the world you created. They don't change it.

What you think and what you feel changes the world. The worst product of an excuse is to focus more energy on a negative outcome and thereby produce more similar results. An alibi is a weak attempt to justify a negative result. Rather than justify - use the power at your command to produce a different result, to succeed, and to succeed wildly.

Excuses are a means to forsake responsibility and surrender power. It is time for you to seize control of your power and your life.

Your journey is what YOU MAKE IT through your thoughts and feelings!

Jessie B. Rittenhouse composed this poem about how life works:

The Wage

I bargained with Life for a penny,
And Life would pay no more,
However I begged at evening
When I counted my scanty store.
For Life is a just employer,
He gives you what you ask,
But once you have set the wages,

Why, you must bear the task.

I worked for a menial's hire,

Only to learn dismayed,

That ANY WAGE I ASKED OF LIFE,

Life would have willingly paid.

You set life's wages. You fix the price for your labor. By way of the thoughts you entertain and the feelings you create, you bargain for success.

Napoleon Hill recognized the link between thought and achievement. He saw the potential every person possesses. He summed up that potential best in the statement: "What you conceive and believe you can achieve." This is not a new idea. The concept is expressed repeatedly in scripture. The Gospel of Mark reassures us, "All thing are possible to the one who believes."

Belief is a matter of thought applied in action. Belief is what we live by.

Ours is a creative reality. Every aspect of creation, including thought, offers, allows, or produces opportunities to feel. Every thought, every feeling is an expression of energy. That energy, once applied, becomes a cause. And for every cause there in an effect. Thoughts and feelings in turn contribute to the speed, direction and outcomes of experience. Thoughts and feelings are the seeds of creation in a never-ending cycle.

Thought impulses in your mind immediately begin to translate themselves into their physical equivalents. The more energy you focus, the more powerful the manifestation.

THOUGHT is the key - your THOUGHTS!!!

THE FOUR HORSEMEN OF THE APOCALYPSE

Riding with you on your journey of life are four horsemen. These riders are the four horsemen of your apocalypse. These are the destructive forces you cultivate in your mind - in the space between truth and action - that lead you astray.

They are: ARROGANCE, FEAR, COMPLACENCY, and CONFUSION.

All four are aspects of the same obstacle - an impediment you create, you feed, you nurture in your mind keeping you from victory, triumph, success. These riders are evident when you resist life, and when you refuse to move in the right and best direction for your growth, your experience, your feeling. The four horsemen of your personal apocalypse dissuade and discourage you from your true path. Free yourself of these riders.

Arrogance is the unbridled surety that one perspective, one viewpoint, is the right one. Relying on a physical, tangible sense of power, the arrogant move themselves and those they influence in the wrong direction. Beware of unbridled hubris. Arrogance is always a function of ignorance or fear.

Fear is a state of mind and a condition that people encourage or censure in their thoughts. Fear is anticipation of pain or loss; faith in the wrong, a negative, outcome. If you fear something, that thing has power over you. Fear is the aspect of being that resists change. Only by acting despite fear do you overcome it. Act with faith in a positive result and succeed.

Complacency is satisfaction with the status quo and with the way things are. In the complacent the motive to act is weak. Here settling trumps desire and laziness trumps effort. The complacent, content, and satisfied refuse to move forward. There is no external remedy for lack of ambition.

Confusion is the refusal to hear the still, small voice within. Confusion results when people dismiss feelings that are pointing to a better way. Overwhelmed by the hustle and bustle of this physical world, by the noise and commotion, people mistakenly believe they are weak, cut off and alone. Lost and confused people put faith in agents and activities leading them astray.

Every choice to deviate from the right path, however, is an opportunity to learn and to grow. In the end, life overpowers all confusion. Don't resist or deny the guides that continually urge you to move in the right direction. Knowing obstacles exist, you are halfway to overcoming them.

Are you disposed to succeed?

Which of these two perspectives most strikes a chord?

1) The world is a dangerous, intimidating, scary place. Life is cold, nasty, brutish and short. My journey through life is lonely and difficult. I am lost, confused and weak. All of life is suffering. Other people are more often a cause of pain than a means of joy. Life has no purpose, no meaning, no certainty. The only thing I could like better than today, is what I knew yesterday. Progress and prosperity are a matter of luck - the toil of fate. Life is destined to end as it began - in a painful, disorienting burst. What comes next? Nothing.

Or

2) The world is a beautiful, inviting, stimulating place. Life is an exhilarating adventure, a challenge, a game. My journey is one of collective discovery and growth. Though I may not see all things clearly, something guides me, strengthens

me, invigorates me. While I may stumble and experience temporary pain, the overarching emotion of my life is joy. Life has a meaning, a purpose, a certainty. While I have enjoyed and learned from the past I celebrate the present, for my life is always on the bridge between past and future. I look forward to new experiences, new discoveries, new growth to come. My life is in my hands. A divine purpose put me here and a divine purpose guides me forever forward. Life is destined to end as it began - as a transition from one state of being to another. I welcome whatever comes next.

If you are not embracing the second perspective, you have work to do.

Fear of ideas is the greatest hindrance to human progress and happiness. Don't let arrogance or fear, complacency or confusion keep you from embracing the truth and changing your life for the better. Make your journey a thrilling adventure.

Behind you is infinite power. Before you lies endless possibility. Around you is boundless opportunity. Why should you fear?

EXPRESSING WISDOM

Here are other words and statements expressing the wisdom you seek. Highlight or circle the declarations that strike you most.

The SECRET OF SUCCESS (move beyond the words, embrace the meaning):

ASK and you will receive;
SEEK and you will find;
KNOCK and the door will open.

CREATE in your mind a burning desire and set out to achieve it.

*CONQUER self and force life to pay
whatever is asked.*

Win by THINKING you can.

Succeed by BECOMING success conscious.

*All things come to you if you have the will
to TRY and the faith to BELIEVE.*

*CREATE the opportunity; the adventure of
your life.*

*FOCUS will and thought, the twin powers
of life.*

FOLLOW one aim.

*SEE your goal steadily, AIM for it
unswervingly.*

SERVE the divine will.

*To get what you've never had, DO what
you've never done.*

STRIVE, SEEK, FIND; never yield.

*To improve your circumstances, IMPROVE
yourself.*

You will be what you WILL to be.

*MAKE your purpose the central focus of your
thought.*

*To conquer failure CONQUER doubt and
fear.*

*Dream lofty dreams, and so you shall
BECOME.*

*KEEP your hand firmly on the helm of
thought.*

*MAKE a strong EFFORT
to produce a great result.*

Nothing happens until something MOVES.

To change the things you look at, CHANGE the way you look at things.

You CREATE your own experience.

Consciously CHOOSE and DIRECT your thoughts.

Desire ATTRACTS results.

What you HOLD in your mind you ATTRACT.

Thoughts ATTRACT like circumstances.

Thoughts MANIFEST in your reality.

You GET what you THINK about.

Deliberately CHOOSE the experiences you MAKE.

FOCUS on how you feel, not on results.

NURTURE desire, CULTIVATE belief.

ALIGN with source energy.

IMAGINE and MAKE it real.

Deliberately CREATE.

ALLOW abundance.

HOLD a definite purpose with unwavering faith.

BELIEVE to create, ACT to receive.

Love what you DO; DO what you love.

The secret of success, though here expressed in many ways, consists of two basic components: action and faith - movement and direction. Your faith resides in your aim. What you live by, you believe. That which you hold in your mind, and feel in your heart, is energy creating the experience you enjoy or endure.

Highlighted in each phrase in the preceding list is a word emphasizing action (movement). Life is a journey. You are on the ride. You have a choice to steer, to resist, or to be carried along. To take responsibility for your life, to claim your power, you must choose to grab the reins - to steer - to take conscious control of the reality you manifest.

Your direction is key. To succeed in life, you must move in the right direction.

The ultimate power - divine will - infinite intelligence - the source - God - moves all life. It urges, no, it demands life flourish, life progress, life fulfills its ultimate purpose. You have a hand in achieving that aim - you are party to that divine will, infinite intelligence. The source fuels you, prods you, and offers you unlimited opportunities. Your part is to feel your way.

Advance in step with divine will. Resisting is futile, as the divine will intends for you only complete fulfillment and pure joy. Any resistance becomes an opportunity to grow, to choose again. You can, as many times as you like, opt for another lesson. You will eventually learn and rejoice in that learning.

Life is motion. You are constantly moving, evolving, becoming. Don't resist life. Move with life. Move with divine will, with infinite intelligence. Move in the right direction. Your focus leads you; your feelings guide you. You create your own reality. Your thoughts manifest. Your feelings tell you if your thoughts are correct - are the best option. By choosing the thoughts to energize you choose the direction you move.

Your speed advancing reflects your motivation. The strength of your desire determines the purity of your focus. The more you concentrate your thoughts, the more feelings you generate, and the sooner a new reality manifests. The stronger your focus, the greater your faith, and the faster the circumstances you desire come into your awareness.

This is how life works. It is the law. You cannot break the law of life.

The SECRET OF SUCCESS:

MOVE IN THE RIGHT DIRECTION!

Choose the right, the best thought. Guide your thoughts to produce the best feelings you can, then allow life to manifest. By choosing better-feeling thoughts, you think and grow.

Act on faith. You grow larger than your current place by cultivating feelings of gratitude and feelings of love. Move your life forward with a fixed purpose. Move with the intention of life to fuller functioning.

Remember, you are not alone. If you want to help yourself, help other people increase.

Ask, believe, receive. Asking is doing something (moving). Asking also sets a direction. You will receive what you ask for. If what you ask for is not in your best interest, you will receive an opportunity to choose again.

Ultimately life is an inside job. You work on the external effects by focusing the internal cause. It's only really work if you don't enjoy it. And if you don't enjoy it, you are doing something wrong.

Awaken to the potential of your power. Your life is an opportunity to experience - to feel. Through your experiences and feelings you contribute to life. Why waste an instant on creating bad feelings?

You want to be happy, we all do. Create happiness every day and always. Life is a feeling; happiness is a feeling. Produce good feelings. Diligent practice will lead to pure joy - pure happiness - pure love. There is no greater success.

The secret of success is the meaning of success. Moving in the right direction brings all the best of life into your awareness. You experience that goodness; you reinforce that goodness; you grow that goodness. Your success is guaranteed.

DO YOU SEE IT NOW?

Does something seem to be holding you back? Only one thing holds us back from our greatest good. We'll get to that in a later chapter.

Have you experienced fleeting moments of great clarity, of calm assurance, of uninhibited joy? If you can answer yes to this question, then you have felt the divine will - infinite intelligence. Listen to it.

You possess talents, aptitude, flair, vision, genius beyond your knowing. You have access to a power that you can harness, what seems to be elusive attributes and magical powers. You have at your command far-reaching forces. You just must make a choice.

You can choose to take control of the power held out for you, or you can leave that power uncontrolled, undisciplined. You can give it away. You access that power by way of your thoughts. Focus your thoughts on a worthwhile aim. Act as if that aim is already manifest and it will be. All things come to you by way of your faith - by what you believe.

You have, you are, a gift to the world. You are a magnificent being, manifesting in a physical reality. The talents you possess are intended for others to savor. Unleash those talents.

All things, all people, all environments contribute to your success. Unlock the mystery of your life. Choose a direction - the best feeling direction - and advance. The thoughts you harbor, the thoughts you empower, control your experience. Choose noble, fulfilling thoughts - thoughts that produce positive, enjoyable, loving experiences. As you do, the road you travel leads you to beauty, to peace, to more joy.

Many have longed to find the truth to fulfill their destiny and realize their full potential. By seeking, you find. You seek the insight, the understanding, the knowledge to begin life anew. In seeking, you enlist the will to persevere. In seeking, you embody the strength to overcome. In seeking, you embrace the courage to proceed. Accept the truth.

Thought is the lever to lift the weight of the world from your shoulders. Fulfill your potential!

The secret of success is to move in the right direction. You move by means of the thoughts you choose, you nurture, you cultivate. Choose your thoughts wisely.

Employing the truth will bring you all things in the measure you desire in the measure you deserve. Recognize these truths; internalize the truths.

Know the truth, and the truth will set you free.

3
ONLY ONE OBSTACLE

Overcoming the only obstacle
to achieving ultimate success!

Oh Lord, remember not only the men and
women of good will,
but also those of ill will.
But do not remember them for the suffering
they inflict,
rather, remember the fruits we bear.
Thanks to this suffering –
our comradeship, our loyalty, our humanity,
our courage, our generosity,
and greatness of heart grows from all of this;
when they come to judgment let all the fruits
we have borne
be their forgiveness.

- Author Known Only to God -

You've heard and read, probably a number of times, that life comes down to "one thing." Seemingly the idea that life, or success in life, only depends on one thing suggests life is simple, life is easy, life is effortless. This makes sense if the one thing is simple, easy, and effortless. Then, life is simple, easy, and effortless for those who abide by the one simple, easy, effortless thing - consistently and continuously.

But what if the one thing is not so simple? What if the one thing is complicated, challenging, and unnerving?

Summarizing the vastness, the opportunity, the diversity of life, or the means of optimizing the experience of life, in one word usually nets a word with varied and complex meanings. Or the guidance itself is circular in expression - that is, the answer is self-evident or points right back to the solution. The value of the summary then is dubious at best.

By way of an obvious example, one version of a singular solution is expressed: "To set the world record in sprints, run faster than everyone else." The runner only has to do one thing and that one thing results in achieving the objective. That statement is correct, but it doesn't help.

In pondering life, self-evident answers are wholly inadequate - usually and especially when they come down to one thing. The other fault of singular answers is that those words (that one thing) have multiple dimensions. It's easy to say life is about "love," or the key to life is "to love." That is one thing. The difficulty arises putting meaning to the word "love." Then "loving" doesn't seem quite so simple; quite so easy, quite so effortless.

I've said this to bring to the forefront the objections to the ideas that are the focus of this chapter and the next. I believe we, you and I, and every other person on this planet, face one and only one obstacle to living a full, fulfilling, and extraordinary life. We will consider that one thing - the one obstacle - in this chapter. So, you might say, we will be focusing on the negative here - the one thing holding us back. In the next chapter we are going to focus on the one thing that can propel us forward. We will focus on the positive. Overcoming the obstacle and leveraging the propellant are the surest way to succeed in life.

In both cases, neither action, focus, nor proposal meet the requirements of simple, easy, and effortless. As with any skill or condition in life, only by mastering the skill or achieving the condition does life become simple, easy, and effortless. Till then, we have work to do.

WHERE ARE YOU NOW?

Is something holding you back? I've posed these questions before. Do you experience, or have you experienced, moments of greatness when you have realized you possess talents, aptitude, flair, vision, genius?

If only you could harness these apparently elusive qualities you could enjoy the prosperity, the abundance, the favor of this magnificent world - the favor so many others savor. The truth is that all things, all people, all environments are here to contribute to your success. Everyone and everything are here for your fulfillment. But, alas - you face one obstacle.

One obstacle stands between you and all the praise, all the prosperity, and ultimate fulfillment. You must overcome one obstacle to fulfill your mission in life and become the person you are destined to be.

Many, like you, struggle and search, hoping to find the key to unlock the mystery of life. Many have longed to find the secret to fulfill their destiny and realize their full potential here and now. You seek to find the lever that will lift the burden from your back or provide you strength to more readily bear it. You seek the insight, the understanding, and the knowledge to begin life on a more prosperous, joy-filled path. By seeking you reinforce the will to persevere. By seeking you embody the strength to overcome. By seeking you embrace the courage to proceed. Ultimately you will realize the wisdom to find your way.

Let these words stir you heart and steel your resolve.

You will recognize the promise, fulfill your potential, and succeed as you have never succeeded before. Since moving in the right direction is the secret to success, moving in the wrong direction is what we should seek to avoid.

What we are talking about here as "the one obstacle" is the thing to move away from and the thing to avoid. By moving in the right direction, we overcome the obstacle and it diminishes in size.

The truth be told, however, the obstacle is a condition of life. The obstacle is evident and accessible as long as you live. But it need not stop you or limit your advance. By overcoming one obstacle you realize true and lasting joy - for yourself and for those you love. Discover how. Read on.

THE MYSTERY

In trying to understand life and determine the way to succeed, people search for answers to a puzzle. The greatest intellects in history have struggled with this puzzle. Thoughtful, insightful, motivated people continue to struggle with the same intellectual conundrum today.

The ultimate enigma is wrapped in these questions (questions we have considered already):

What is the meaning of life?

Why am I here?

What am I to do?

How far can I go?

How do I achieve my full potential?

While words can help on this quest, words can comfort and words can guide, no one can answer these questions for you. The answer to these questions is in the living of your life.

While countless people grapple still with these fundamental problems, humble sages and saints discovered the truth ages ago. Realizing the simplicity and beauty of the truth they didn't worry about it, they didn't dissect it; they *lived* it. A few unassuming souls order their lives by the truth still today. The wise recognize the promise in this life. The wise, by way of their persistent questioning, their earnest listening, and their willingness to receive, have solved the puzzle. The truly wise have answered the riddle. They have found a way out of the maze.

Ultimately the wise accept where they are and find joy in it. They act faithfully to complete the task before them. They give the full measure of their attention to the chore at hand. By working through life, by acting in a certain way, by persevering and persisting, they fulfill their mission in life.

For the enlightened, life is not a mystery to solve, it's an experience to embrace - an adventure to live - an activity to enjoy. The wise recognize the obstacle to fulfillment, and naturally or deliberately act to overcome it. You too can be wise and live an enlightened life. You can truly prosper here and now. Sit quietly and listen closely to the still, small voice within...

Here again, begin with the end in mind.

WHAT IS SUCCESS?

We've covered this ground before. I am not intent on beating a dead horse, just reinforcing an important point. So, please bear with me as we sow these fertile fields once more.

The word "success" is a transformative word. Success does not endure in time and space. Achieving a task is but a temporary stop, a momentary pause, along a never ending journey. Once someone attains something, new goals and new ambitions arise, and a new quest begins.

As life is change, success essentially means this: life is different in a positive way from how it was yesterday. Success means moving toward, working toward, journeying toward something better, something more. Some people, though, consider success a plateau. For these people success is having achieved or acquired some position or condition in life. Most often this means possessing a certain degree of affluence, having acquired a measure of education or status, and or having compiled a list of accomplishments (in any single field or in a variety of fields). These people rely on past achievements as evidence that they have arrived and now occupy what they deem to be a successful position.

Others, those with less lofty expectations, also settle; they just settle for less. Their plateau is a modicum of security with a dash of comfort. These people are getting by - they are surviving. And they don't aspire to much more, at least not with enough enthusiasm to do anything about it.

Like with everything in this world, however, success - or a station on any plateau - is only temporary. You travel, you arrive, you celebrate, you journey on. If success is not the route you navigate, it will endure for an instant and then pass away. Clinging to anything (stuff, people, conditions) in a dynamic reality is both exhausting and foolhardy. Life is change, life is movement. Resisting is pointless.

For one still seeking to live, still seeking to get more out of life, still seeking to fulfill his or her ultimate potential, previous successes are stepping stones already traversed. Past experiences contributed to making you the person you are now. Success is found in continuing to move, continuing to climb, continuing to advance.

Life is dynamic, success is dynamic. When you stop moving, you've reached the end (figuratively at first, but eventually literally as well). Success, either in a moment of triumph, victory or achievement, or in the ongoing effort of an attempt, is always a feeling. Everything in life represents, stimulates, or calls forth a feeling. Everything external, upon breaching your awareness causes a feeling. Life is feeling. Success is pursuing and realizing good feelings.

Success, like life, is transformative. Each word (success and life) allows and expresses a vast array of meanings (the "one thing" predicament). In limited dimensions we can consider success across a continuum (an alternative depiction of THE SUCCESS SPECTRUM). In one direction wealth (stuff, possessions) and social status lead to ignorance, anxiety, longing, and despair. In the other direction growth and understanding lead to wisdom, peace, fulfillment, and love. Material possessions and social status need not necessarily lead to angst, but focusing on status or wealth serves most often as a stumbling block - a means to resist life's greatest good and highest intention. Focusing on stuff or status causes us to move in the wrong direction.

WEALTH   SOCIAL STATUS   GROWTH   UNDERSTANDING

IGNORANCE
ANXIETY
LONGING   FEAR ●●◀━━━━━●━━━━━▶●● FAITH
DESPAIR

WISDOM
PEACE
FULFILLMENT
LOVE

PHYSICAL, TANGIBLE   ETHEREAL, SPIRITUAL
TEMPORARY   ENDURING

◀━━━━━   ━━━━━▶
        WHAT HOLDS YOU BACK   WHAT LIFE INTENDS

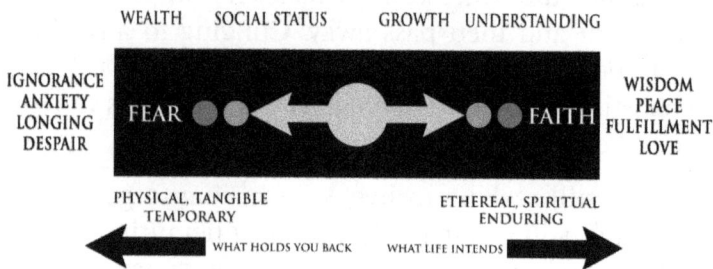

MOVE IN THE RIGHT DIRECTION

Wealth (Material Possessions) - Social Status - Wisdom and Enlightenment

Immersed in a material world people, not surprisingly, gravitate to tangible things - to property and possessions - as what they have come to believe is the prime measure of success. Since we attach our desires to things, by acquiring those objects of desire, we elicit feelings of accomplishment, feelings of esteem, feelings of power. We mistake those transient ego-feelings as success.

People are inclined to exhibit a genuine disconnect when exploring this topic - the meaning of success. When questioned about what success means, people tend to shy away from material possessions and accumulation as definitions. Most individuals, invariably, express more esoteric notions of success - that success is transformative, is fulfilling. Behavior, however, illuminates a different conclusion.

Watching what people *do*, as opposed to what people *say*, reveals their true beliefs. In a material world, in a consumer driven commercial society, wealth is afforded a unique and honored status. People in their hearts recognize wealth is not the highest good; they just have trouble overcoming the predominant current - the need to have, possess, and acquire more. We are, after all, social creatures, so we succumb to social pres-

Success 101: How Life Works

sure. As we see others accumulate we believe getting and having stuff must be "the answer." A part of each of us wants to compete and win.

In our modern, affluent society, possessions are the obvious external trappings of success. They are seen as the route to coveted feeling of success. People often conclude that success in a physical world means mastering the physical. In a consumer society we demonstrate mastery by accumulating stuff. Consumers tend to believe more stuff means more feelings of success.

Feelings of power and status, masquerading as success, are typically achieved by means of wealth - property and possessions. We seek to own or control assets of all kinds. Even toys become the goal - the route to feelings we seek. Wealth through financial assets allows people a measure of freedom - freedom from worry over financial issues and freedom to devote time, energy and talent to what they love. The wealthy can travel when and where they want. They can do what they want, when they want. They can stay in luxurious accommodations and have people cater to their every whim.

Where most people aspire to wealth, having it allows another aspect of success. Wealth is accorded influence and worldly power. Influence is a factor of status and stature - respect and esteem within a family, a group, or a community. Wealth is not required to wield influence. Influence can be had through a number of means: moral, religious, legal, or positional authority, relationships (knowing the right people; having cultivated trust), physical stature, and so on. While wealth is not necessary for influence, in a culture driven by money, having wealth or influence (controlling what others covet) automatically affords the possessor a position of power.

Wealth and status are false idols. Success is always a feeling - a good feeling, a true feeling, an enduring feeling. Success is setting on the right course. Wealth and status (mastery of the physical world and the means of creation) may be a byproduct of moving in the right direction, but they never satisfy in the end. Now let's consider other dimensions of success.

Think about the individual who accumulates wealth and achieves a position of status. All that property and temporal power are of little consolation if that person lacks health. A key dimension of success is health – feeling good; being fit and trim; athletic; free of disease and capable of staying that way. Physical and mental well-being (health) are the foundation upon which a fantastic life journey is built. Physical and mental well-being are not mandatory for success in life, but compared to wealth and status, health is priceless.

Then we have the dimension of physical appearance. Beauty is an attribute often associated with success and is often equated with a condition of health. Some people (mostly women) strive for beauty as an ultimate goal in itself. For these people, an attractive appearance, though not everything, is imperative. For others, beauty is a consequence of attaining and maintaining health in mind and body.

For some, fame and notoriety are synonymous with success. While renown may be achieved as recognition for some talent or accomplishment or unique and extraordinary action completed, for an untold number of people the objective is to achieve celebrity by any means. Being recognized and known famously or infamously is sufficient to claim success. Fame brings its own brand of influence.

Success can be through intellectual pursuits. The accumulation of knowledge, the attainment of education, the intellectual mastery of a discipline are all productive endeavors. People explore, they grow, they expand their understanding, and in so doing succeed. While knowledge alone does not connote power, knowledge is an asset. Knowledge and understanding are useful ingredients and valuable resources to employ along the journey of life. Accumulating knowledge and then applying that knowledge can facilitate the journey of success. Applying knowledge generates power and can be a path to wisdom.

The journey of a thousand miles, the passage through life, is not a solitary journey. At some point, usually sooner rather than later, most people come to realize success in life is a factor of relationships. The nature of life - our biology, our genetics, our hormones - brings us together. We are social creatures, living a communal experience. Life seeks to expand and we each contribute. Every aspect of life is determined, promoted, or enhanced by positive relationships. The opposite is also true: every aspect of life is distorted, discouraged, or destroyed by negative relationships.

An individual cannot feel safe or secure but in relation to other people. A person cannot belong or experience love without others. A person cannot achieve a position of stature or esteem without other people. A solitary life is one reduced to lonely wanderings; to confrontations and competition; to trial; and in the end tragedy. Success by any complete measure requires other people. Success requires relationships.

As social beings, our success is measured through a great marriage or romantic bond; intimacy between caring people; happy, well-adjusted, independent and prosperous children; and admiring, or at least supportive, family members, friends and colleagues. No one achieves anything alone; no one succeeds alone. Success is never, nor can ever be, an individual attainment. Success is a collective achievement, a cooperative effort. Human beings succeed together.

The final dimension of success to consider here is spiritual. Enlightenment, or spiritual success, encompasses all the other dimensions of success.

The enlightened accepts and enjoys the physical world, but moves beyond material wealth. The enlightened is free, and possesses ultimate personal power. The enlightened warrants a unique standing among human beings, but has no desire for status or fame. The enlightened understands the simple and profound truth that is sufficient to fulfill his or her purpose for living. The enlightened embraces life in communion with others, but does not rise or fall on the opinions, perceptions, or aspirations of those people. A meaningful purpose, the energy and motivation to keep moving toward that purpose, and the conviction that the direction is true, bring fulfillment, bring joy, bring peace. The enlightened operate in this space.

Reaching the pinnacle of success - achieving spiritual success - elicits a transformation in life. Realizing spiritual success transforms existence from drudgery to celebration, from trial to triumph, from anxiety to peace. The whole world changes for the one who sees it from the highest peak - a perspective of genuine truth.

How do you define "success" for you?

What makes you feel successful?

As mentioned, in our modern, material society, we equate success with "things." Our nature of constantly striving, constantly desiring, causes us to determine that success means "more" things. We often equate prosperity to having more – more stuff: property, possessions, relationships, prestige. "Having more" is what life is about. The irresistible force in every living thing desires to have more life - more experiences, more feeling. We just tend to get turned around, and head in the wrong direction. Instead of positive experiences producing energizing feelings, we choose negative experiences that drain us. Instead of doing more, experiencing more, and becoming more, we busy ourselves accumulating more, and bide our time, lamenting a lack of wonder in life. Mistaken in our understanding of success, we pursue insufficient ends, with insufficient means. We misdirect our time, our talents, and our energy heading for the wrong goal.

You are guaranteed to get "more" in life - what will you choose? More good or more bad?

No matter where you are in life at this moment, don't think you have failed. Each detour you took was an opportunity and a chance to grow. If the situation brought negative feelings, it was an occasion to recognize you could choose better. You are at another decision point now. Before you lies an opportunity to grow, to change course, to feel. While your wayward route may have delayed you, and you may face challenges still, understand what success truly is:

> Success is ultimately a feeling.
>
> Success is a feeling of joy.
>
> Success is expansion, growth.
>
> Success is more - more life.

The courage we desire and prize we seek is not the courage to die decently, but to live fully.

- THOMAS CARLYLE -

THE OBSTACLE

In life, one obstacle diverts us from the optimum path.

That one obstacle, one barrier, one impediment, causes us to squander our energy, waste our talents, and diffuse our focus. Every time we succumb to the power of the obstruction, we fail to fulfill our true potential.

Every human being faces the same obstacle. Every human being since time immemorial faced the same obstacle. Everyone has been misled. Everyone has been deceived.

The obstacle keeps us from taking a direct path to our greatest good. That misdirection, however, is not without purpose. By facing the obstacle and dealing with the diversion, we learn about ourselves and learn about life. The pain we endure makes us stronger and allows us to grow. The difficulties we confront make the inevitable victory that much more sweet.

Every person must deal with the obstacle in their own way, in their own good time. While the obstacle may have detained you, or may be challenging you still, you can get past it. You can move on to your ultimate success.

We, you and I, are observers of an earthly drama and dreamers of a grand dream. Despite all the trappings of this life, we each are individual portals observing, sensing, experiencing an infinite unfolding kaleidoscope of life. We are observers experiencing this reality, yet we live what we think we are. Instead of accepting a "self" as an unencumbered observer frolicking in the playground, we fall prey to the one and only obstacle to ultimate success: *Ego.*

Ego is the snare of the human condition. Ego leads us from tranquility to turmoil, from cooperation to competition, from abundance to scarcity. Ego implores, berates, condemns us to believe we are separate from the environment, separate from each other, and separate from what is. By placating ego, we invite pain into our lives.

Ego clings to the body and what the body can sense.

Ego embraces physical reality, dismissing out of hand any alternative to what it can see, touch, and manipulate. Ego, though intended to be servant, seeks to be master. Ego makes the dream real, and at times, if we let it, turns that dream into a nightmare.

Unleashed, the ego intends to dominate; to define a separate self, a self apart and distinct from all else, a self that would be king. One thoughtful seeker, Wayne Dyer, sums up ego as six ideas:

1. I am what I have.

2. I am what I do.

3. I am my reputation.

4. I am separate from you.

5. I am separate from what is.

6. I am separate from God.

A Course in Miracles explains the power of ego as, "We are asleep, dreaming that we are separate from God." That aspect of self that sees an "I" as separate, seeks to exalt that "I."

Ego seeks to control, to dominate, and in so doing "be" something. By surrendering to ego we lose contact with our essence, our awareness. We lose feeling, we lose vision, we squander our ability to choose for our highest good. Answering to ego, we lose our freedom, we forego our power.

Ego defines a "me" and craves control. Ego seeks to rule, and it believes that by so doing it secures its immortality. Our folly lies in yielding to the beguiling message of ego. Instead of controlling the tool (meant to help navigate this physical reality), we submit to ego's will. We allow the servant to master.

The seminal weapon of ego is the double-edged sword. One blade is fear and the other is arrogance. When ego wields this sword, both blades cut deep. Fear rules in relationships; we dare not engage lest we face rejection. Fear rules in business; we fail to step up and put our talent to the test lest we confirm we might not be worthy. Fear rules when we dare not act lest we appear the fool and risk loss of status or prestige or respect. Fear weakens and enslaves.

At the opposite extreme is the other face of ego. Here ego rules by intimidation. Pride and conceit are its tools of disillusionment. Ego convinces us we are superior to others - more capable, stronger, more intelligent, more deserving. Through arrogance we come to believe independence is our birthright, our gift, our power. We stand separate because we are better than the great unwashed. We ignore the still, small voice within, and dismiss our own feelings. We know the way.

Ego's weapon threatens your true purpose. Fear and arrogance both undermine and dominate. Lost to ego's power, people tend to seek allies in the world, often with toxic results.

As powerful and threatening the weapon of ego is, you need only remember that you control the weapon. Both fear and arrogance spring up from the ego and are nurtured in the mind. The more you separate yourself from what is, the world and the people around you, the more you succumb to the power of ego. In truth you have but one choice: a choice between freedom and bondage. Freedom is the way of peace, love, and joy - the way to a full and fulfilling life. Bondage, the way of ego, leads to despair.

You are always free to choose.

OVERCOME THE OBSTACLE

The first and most profound choice to succeed in life is to choose opportunity over ego, freedom over bondage, good feelings over bad. When you release yourself from the grip of ego you find peace and joy - positive feelings unparalleled in the forest of ego's illusion.

The most direct, and surest way to overcome ego is to recognize ego's influence. You must learn to recognize when the sword is unsheathed. When you feel fear the ego is influencing you. When you judge and condemn, when you criticize and complain, the blade of arrogance is brandished against your highest purpose.

Release the sword. Let it fall from your grip. You will repeat the lessons of life until you learn ego leads to pain. As observer in, and co-creator of, this unfolding adventure called life, you command a body, a mind, and a will. You employ these faculties within an environment. Choosing the humility of acceptance over the judgment, vengeance and arrogance of ego is the path to freedom, the path to serenity, the path to joy.

Ego causes you to resist the free flow of life. By surrendering to the influence of ego, even a simple act of resistance leads you out of the moment, out of the experience. Ego, that aspect of the body, mind and will seeking to dominate, belabors the past and offers false hope in a flawed future. Ego misleads you all the while looking for, longing for, a time and circumstance to dominate - a time to take charge, an opportunity to take control.

To experience freedom and peace, you must not allow ego to dominate your life. You must accept who you are, what you are, and the circumstances of your existence. You are a creative, powerful being. You are on an exciting journey of adventure, of experience, of feeling.

When ego rears its head, recognize your culpability in its rising. In those instances, in those circumstances you separate yourself from the source. You venture alone in a world cast in shadow. You need not venture alone.

Only by heeding wisdom's soft call, that still, small voice within, will you come to understand you are watching "B-grade" movies all the while with the remote control in hand. Change the channel. By accepting life in the present, you shake ego. You are ultimately responsible. Ego is not in charge. Do not allow ego to gain control. Once you accept full responsibility for what you have, who you are, and what you do, will you understand that the beguiling message ego offers is a lie. You are not separate, you are not alone, you have nothing to fear.

Embrace the paradox: Accept responsibility for what seems beyond your control.

As you live your life you provide an individual perspective and experience of this existence. You are not separate from all that is, nor are you alone on the journey. Ego is about "me," "I," and "self." It is selfish, self serving, and fearful. Divorce yourself from ego. Move away from ego to recognize that life is about "we," "us," and "everyone." You are not separate. You are not alone.

Life allows individual experiences, individual feelings - these are experiences and feelings we share. Life is a collective purpose, a collective journey. Your life, my life - your experiences, your feelings; my experiences, my feelings - are all different aspects of a unified whole. We play out the joys and sorrows, the trial and triumphs, the challenges and hopes together.

Your success in life, your feelings of joy, of compassion, of love, are feelings we all share. Your success is a cause to celebrate and rejoice. Everyone's success in life is a cause to celebrate and rejoice. In the illusion of this physical reality we mistakenly fall prey to ego. Each of us has a body, a mind, and a will. We each appear to be on our own separate course. The truth appears to be a paradox: we live and work, play and pray as individuals, but we are part of a grand symphony - a collective adventure. The story is bigger than "me." By embracing the paradox, denying self (ego) and accepting full and total responsibility for the quality of your experience, you liberate yourself.

Some power greater than self animates this existence; that power has brought you to the crossroads of energy and intention - to life. You have the wondrous opportunity to create, to move, and to feel. The best choice, the most appealing choice, is to choose good feelings over bad, to choose joy over sorrow, to choose exhilaration over complacency. Your mission is to feel – so why not feel wonderful?

For your part, you are that still watcher - the observer - taking in the experience, feeling the emotions, and feeling the outcome of choices. You navigate the environment and, in concert with a higher power, you have a hand in creating the experience. The circumstances you face and the environment you find yourself in are both ultimately of your own creation. You are not separate from what is, but rather one with what is. Overcoming the limitation of ego is the key. Move in the right direction.

Reduced to its simplest measure, come to understand that you have but one choice: a choice between freedom or bondage. Freedom is accepting the lessons of life and the wisdom of creation. Bondage is empowering ego and resisting life.

Put another way: your choice is either to accept or resist. You have power when you realize everything that exists outside and around your self is the product of that choice, and is of your making. To experience complete freedom, assume complete responsibility for your life. Accept responsibility, reject ego, and listen to that still, small voice inside guiding you and telling you that the way is easy, the burden is light. Humility empowers your true nature and is the way to wisdom.

There is no more to wisdom than this:
Accept the grace of God.

To master ego, accept two seemingly paradoxical conditions:

1. The master plan is beyond understanding and is greater than intellect.

2. You are totally responsible for your life, all that happens, and all that is.

This notion leaves quite a quandary. You can't understand the plan - the workings, purpose and destiny of this reality - yet you are totally and completely responsible for your experience of it.

Accept total responsibility for all that is, and all that happens, and realize the truth that none of it is real, none of it matters. You are along for the ride. Make it a joyous ride.

Declaring you are completely and totally responsible is one thing; believing, and therefore living it, is another. To go from the skepticism, fear, and self-righteousness of ego to truth requires conditioning yourself to step back from the emotion of the moment. You must recognize and realize circumstances are what they are, and that is all. The desires you entertained yesterday, and the choices you made yesterday, produced what you experience today. If you want to change what you experience next, choose again. Choose a better course.

Every moment, every action, every interaction is an opportunity to disempower ego and empower spirit. Every time you choose better feelings of connectedness and joy, you learn; you move closer to ultimate reality and you align with divine intelligence. You move in the right direction.

To neutralize the double-edged sword of ego, accept that all is right with the world - it's okay. Rain, wind, snow; rich, poor; educated, uneducated, it's all okay. The circumstances of life are neither "someone's" nor "the system's" fault. There is no victim. There is no one to blame. This lesson is offered until this truth is accepted. We are not separate; we are masters of our fate.

Your choice is to accept or resist - to be in harmony (at peace) or in conflict (ego's temporary illusion of power). Ultimately, the end is not in doubt; you choose the amount of pain suffered in the illusion as you journey to wholeness. The struggle is only and forever in your mind.

What is, is. For what will be, you have two choices: go with ego or go with life. Accept the master plan; humbly rejoice in every circumstance as awakening your responsibility to choose and your opportunity to feel.

Wherever ego looks, it sees conflict and division, pain and oppression. Ego's tools are hubris and fear. To move from the tempest to the calm, from trial to peace, from guilt to innocence, invest the talent and energy at your disposal to recognize the world for what it is - a fanciful unfolding and a grand opportunity. To embrace the true, enduring reality, forgive those you perceive as trespassing against you. Forgive the circumstances and events you perceive to be conspiring against you. By letting go of the conflict of the illusion you ultimately forgive yourself.

Remember: "I am responsible" and "Forgiveness comes from forgiving."

THE WAY IS SIMPLE

Life is to be lived.

Even if you tend to believe you are journeying through the valley of death, your final destination is the safety of a warm embrace and loving home. To get to that destination do not squander your life, nor spend it frivolously; invest what you have in the lives of others.

To invest life, you must share unencumbered by guilt. What you experience, what you feel fuels us all. Choose good feelings. For peace to reign, forgive - all and always. By joining with others in relationship, in love, you become whole.

Today is not life in the fast lane; it is life in the oncoming lane. Ego puts you in the oncoming lane and accelerates life so that you find it difficult to hear the still, small voice guiding you home. To recognize truth, overcome the obstacles in your mind: "I have been wronged," and "I am unworthy." Both these misperceptions (arrogance and fear) require true forgiveness. The journey from sleep to awakening is made in small steps.

Overcome the hubris of ego by learning to forgive. Refuse to judge, condemn, criticize or complain. Accept responsibility for all you experience. Let go of perceived hurts and perceived injustices. You see, if this life is an illusion, then so are your perceptions of injustice. There is no one to blame and nothing to fear. Forgiving is giving peace, allowing a smile, and inviting laughter despite the circumstances. You are not separate from your creator. You are not alone. You are one - whole, complete, powerful, and loving. You forgive yourself in the same measure as you forgive others.

The promise of life is this: your journey is meant to be one of abundance, excitement, joy, and opportunity.

You have a unique purpose, a unique mission, and unique gifts. To fulfill your grand purpose, to contribute to the grand design - to grow, to learn, to live, to love - to feel alive - overcome ego - that aspect of your being that insists you are alone, separate from others and separate from what is. To succeed in life, master ego.

Overcoming ego and trusting in the truth and beauty of the experience is the difference between life or death, happiness or despair. By facing fear and letting go of the need to judge you learn to forgive. By forgiving you find your place and your purpose in this world. Open yourself to the journey - to the magnificent opportunity.

My prayer for you is that you recognize the promise of this life, and in so doing overcome ego to fulfill your potential!

The truth is, you only have one obstacle to overcome. The obstacle is inside you. Everything you see around you - the challenges, the trials, the confrontations - pale in comparison. The only obstacle to overcome to achieve your full potential is ego.

Choose to overcome the one thing that holds you back.

The choice is always yours.

Make the right choice!

72

Success 101: How Life Works

4

THE ONE THING

Here again is a bold assertion. Success in life boils down to one thing. And I'm not talking about arriving at the destination. I'm not talking about feeling blissful feelings. The one thing that this chapter is devoted to is the one thing you can, should, and must do to live a successful life. Every person has the ability to do this one thing, and the individuals who do make this one thing a priority will head in the right direction. They will live full and fulfilling lives.

EQUAL ASSETS

You may still be wrestling with the idea that somehow you have not been blessed with the capacity for success. Rewarding lives are only for the elect, and you are not among the chosen few. You might think it's only the privileged who succeed: the ones born to wealth, with great looks and high IQs. They have all the advantages, all the resources, all the allies. You might think you don't have the pedigree, the education, or the demeanor to succeed. Well, thinking that success or excellence is for the fortunate few is a misguided notion.

Now we all like to fantasize about "equality." American colonists revolted against a mighty empire to unshackle the bonds restraining their potential and limiting their advance. The leaders of the young republic established a constitution based on ideals of freedom, equality, and opportunity. These ideals rarely exist in the real world.

Freedom is a condition people settle on in doses. True freedom recognizes and exercises ultimate power. That power, however, is accompanied by ultimate responsibility. People, usually, commonly, mostly, are willing to settle for a degree of freedom as opposed to complete and unfettered freedom and the attendant responsibility.

Opportunity is a factor of people striving, building, creating. Opportunities are the coming together of motivation and need. People have or create needs, and people are moved, for various reasons, to fulfill those needs. A society's system, culture, and direction determine its propensity for opportunity. If the culture is stagnant, controlled, or satisfied, opportunity is limited. If the culture is vibrant, free, and eager, opportunities abound. So it is with the individual.

Equality is the interesting notion in this holy triumvirate cited here. Equality has no basis in physical reality. In America we speak of equality in terms of treatment and consideration, or openness to opportunity. We deem things equal if they are "close enough." That is, the things, people, environments are equal if comparative factors are of similar or equal measure.

The truth, which our politically correct society chooses to avoid, is that people are different.

No two human beings - no two people - are exactly alike. No two people see things exactly the same way, exhibit the same preferences, and possess the same potential. Human beings are more similar than they are different, but they are *not* equal to one another.

Equal doesn't exist in external reality, and that is not a bad state of affairs. Every life is meant to be a unique venture, an exceptional quest, an incomparable journey. Every person is moved by varying doses of unique motives. Every person experiences a unique perspective from unique circumstances and realizes wholly unique results. This is how life works.

While physical equality only exists in theory, each person is part of the same whole. Each individual has access to assets, resources, motivation, and power to essentially determine that people are "close enough." In a relatively free society we, in fact, have equal opportunity.

Every person has access to, and employs regularly, the power to create the circumstances and the experiences of their lives. People don't have the same DNA and hereditary makeup. They don't have the same skin tone, stature, and looks. They don't have the same voices or coordination or talents. Every person is a "one of a kind," unique, uniquely valuable and capable being. The lifespan and the environments of every individual are different. What they like, what they dislike, what moves them to action is different, but there are some things they get and have access to and use in equal measure with every other being on the planet.

What we measure as a day has twenty-four hours, one thousand four hundred and forty minutes, or 86,400 seconds. Each day is an equal measure for every human being that inhabits this planet. Everyone has the ability to, and will absolutely invest those 86,400 seconds some way.

No one can claim that he or she, or those other people have an advantage when it comes to the number of seconds in a day. We all get the same amount. A lifetime is the accumulation of experience built over using the smallest increments of time. We get thirty-one million, five hundred and thirty-six thousand seconds in a typical year. We get two billion, five hundred and twenty-two million, eight hundred and eighty thousand seconds in a typical life. Are you investing or wasting yours?

We, each and every person, have access to and use consumable assets every day. Researchers have concluded that a typical person generates, experiences, or has between twenty thousand (20,000) and sixty thousand (60,000) thoughts per day. Thoughts range from fleeting impulses, to flashing images, to deliberate focused and empowered concentration, communication, and action. Each brain, each mind is a receiver and a transmitter of seemingly infinite thought.

Choice - the free will that human beings have the ability to exercise - begins and ends in thought. People choose to entertain and empower thought. They choose what impulses, what motives, and what messages they focus on and empower. You might not get to choose every thought that transits you brain waves, but you do get to choose which ones you allow, entertain, and reinforce. You get to choose your thoughts.

Thought is an element that exists both in and beyond this dimension. Thought is power. Thought is energy, creative energy. Every thought influences and directs the molding of experience. Thoughts literally create the reality of human experience. Every person, knowingly or unknowingly, deliberately or unwittingly, exercises, employs or somehow uses twenty to sixty thousand thoughts per day. Those thoughts create the circumstances and experiences of the reality they enjoy or endure.

Where you are and what you experience is not exactly the same as anyone else on this planet. You have a unique role to play. You have been dealt a unique hand. You have a unique opportunity. But you have the exact same assets, the exact same resources, the exact same opportunity to express life as every other person on the planet. The question is, what will your expression be?

Are you seeking a full and fulfilling life, a life of adventure, of accomplishment, of exhilaration, of achievement? Or are you seeking a life of compromise, of calamity, or comfort? Are you seeking to bide your time and wait the ride out, hoping to just survive?

The truth is you are not going to survive this life forever. You have a transient opportunity. Your window of opportunity is renewed each day, but shrinks in relation to the time of your life. Are you going to employ your assets for the greater good? Or are you going to waste them?

The difference as to where someone goes, what someone accomplishes, and who someone becomes ultimately is not a factor of inheritance, or intelligence, or talent; it is a factor of how that individual invests, employs, or otherwise uses his or her assets - his or her thought.

Thought creates the reality you experience. Thought is the creative force - a component part of ultimate power. Through thought humans access the realm of cause - the dimension beyond our own, our realm of effect. How you use your thoughts determines your success in life.

So if thought is your decisive power, and you have a virtually limitless, renewing supply of thoughts, what is the one thing that matters most?

ULTIMATE FOCUS - ULTIMATE POWER

Have you ever taken a magnifying glass and focused sunlight onto your hand? The heat from the concen-

trated rays becomes intense. Focusing even tepid sun-
beams on the right fuel can ignite a raging fire.

Unifying, leveraging, and combining energy produces
overwhelming strength. Concentrating force at the decisive place and time can literally change the course of
history. Focusing, concentrating your power toward a
single-minded purpose, is the surest way to achieve,
to produce, to create any condition, any circumstance,
any objective. The most important task for you, then, is
for you to determine your focus.

You have thousands of assets available to you every day
(thoughts). You are using those assets, perhaps hap-
hazardly, but you are using them nevertheless. Your
thoughts have produced what you have experienced
in your life up to this point. Your thoughts have created the circumstances you face today. The good news
is that every journey to excellence starts from the same
point. It starts from where you are right now. You can
change direction, you can adjust your speed. You can
set your course for a new fulfilling, exhilarating, and
joy-filled destination. You can begin, here and now
to generate momentum, to begin accelerating toward
some worthwhile end. The moment of truth is the moment of decision.

You must decide, choose, commit to focusing your assets. This means committing some time and energy di-
recting thought - your thoughts. Focus your thoughts
to produce favorable circumstances. Ultimate focus
produces ultimate power. Applying your thoughts to
achieve a worthwhile end, one in line with the purpose
and intent of life, which is to grow, will assuredly move
you in a positive, life affirming, life renewing direction.

You are a success when you choose to succeed.

I MUST KNOW "HOW"

Much is made, and more will be covered throughout this book, on how to succeed. Any and every "how" offered is an attempt, albeit and inadequate attempt, to bridge the gap between creator and creation, between thought and result.

Often we human beings resist truth with all our might. Instead we cling tight to what we know and what we experience in physical reality. But what we experience are "effects." We don't understand "cause." We fail to have faith until we are shown how this could be. Faith in the truth, the way of life, is ultimate faith and is ultimate power.

Any person who possesses pure faith - faith unencumbered by doubt and fear - is sure to create and grow. The faithful person is sure to become to a degree far beyond the individual grounded in material reality. To embrace your ultimate potential you must move from fear to faith.

In the fields of faith (as through the traditions of the world's great religions), science, and success we find frequent and constant attempts to bridge the divide between doubt (meaning fear) and truth. Teachers, counselors, authors and leaders attempt to overcome the innate resistance and fear in the hearts of men by suggesting how to use the assets every individual has available. Unfortunately, and often quite easily, some people see and take advantage of people's doubt and fear, indecision and disbelief. These nefarious characters lead the weak-willed further astray.

If people are afraid or unwilling to direct their own thoughts toward worthwhile and fulfilling ends, or if they are anxious or reluctant to discipline their minds to produce valuable creations, others will step in. Manipulators and frauds appear to fill the void of those lost and afraid, the people whose thoughts produce less than positive results.

Since people don't know they possess, or have access to, the ultimate power, or because they are unwilling to bear the ultimate responsibility that accompanies this power, people willingly give their power away. For meager crumbs of bread, modest entertainment, and a modicum of security (all in all a rather cheap price) people are willing to forfeit the opportunity of their lives.

Most people will rely without question on the direction of authority to determine their path, the investment of their assets, and ultimately, the experience of their potential. You and I both know, however, nothing comes without a price. Forfeiting your power of thought leaves you to the whim and the will of those you think that you can trust.

By not thinking for yourself, by not claiming your right and bearing your responsibility, you become a pawn in someone else's plan. You become a laborer for a wage. Yours then becomes "not to question why," and yours becomes "to do and die'" by whatever means the influencer commands.

The truth is, your thoughts determine the quality and the accomplishments of your life. Absolute faith, and absolute focus, produce the best result. You don't need to worry about "how" - you just need the faith, measured in fortitude, measured in focus, measured in thought. What you think about will manifest. What you desire will appear.

You are a creator, intended to contribute to life. You are meant to add to the magnificence. The one thing you can, should, and must do is determine what you want and where you are heading. By way of thought you choose the direction to move. That is the one thing that you control, and that is the one thing that matters most.

You have the means. Do you have the will?

For those still harboring a shred of doubt let us detour to explore and understand "how."

SUCCESS FACTORS

You are a dynamic, infinitely capable being. You possess a host of attributes, skills, and talents. Some of these you recognize and have developed, and some you do not have the slightest clue are within your grasp and within your being.

A common element of the human condition is that while ultimate reality may be whole, few things in this world seem complete and absolute. One of the core messages of this volume is that despite any misgivings, despite any doubts or fears you may harbor, the one thing you can and must do to succeed in life is to take the next step. You must move in a direction you believe will lead you somewhere, even if you still question whether you can and will arrive. Take the next step.

If you must find a "how," then deliberately go to work on yourself. The world will begin to change when you do.

Listed below are the most often cited and suggested talents and attributes of successful people.

Successful people are moving in the right direction. They align their thoughts toward achieving worthwhile objectives. Actions follow from thought. Effects are created from the energy of thoughts and action. In aligning their thoughts, men and women become successful people. Outsiders observe the traits they exhibit and the actions they take and conclude success must be in these traits and these actions. The traits and the actions are the effects of thought.

If jumping from fear to faith, from doubt to truth, is too large a chasm, then initiate the journey where you can. Start with a small step of remaking yourself. Begin to develop the qualities, the attributes, the characteristics of successful people. By beginning to embrace aspects of the "how," you will begin to reveal and arrive at a new conclusion.

Most of us, me included, need to take baby steps to move from fear to faith. But we must take the step. Start behaving like a successful person. Do what successful people do, internalize their propensity to act in a specific way. Through small measures you will begin to change. Start where you are. Choose something you can do now. Take the next step! Think and act - for that is life.

Following are the key attributes and behaviors successful people embody. A useful strategy to employ when undertaking to achieve a significant purpose is to break the large task into smaller, more manageable parts. As you scan through these characteristics, look for one, or a few, you can start to develop for yourself immediately. Even the largest fire begins from a single spark.

Having a Positive Attitude
Your attitude almost always determines your altitude in life. Keep your eyes focused on the light, and shadow will not cross your face. If you are a "glass half empty" type of person, get to work. Deliberately look for the good. Laugh often. Change your attitude to become success conscious.

Enthusiastic, Passionate
Achieving anything of significance requires enthusiasm

and passion. Enthusiasm is from the Greek root for "spirit within." Enthusiasm and passion are energized inspiration, intensity of focus and intensity of effort. Enthusiasm and passion are thought energy translated into action.

Proactive
You are the creator. You are in charge. You are responsible. Seize, retain, and exploit the initiative - the whole world is waiting for you to act. Solve problems. A "problem" is an internal definition, so act accordingly. Problems fall into three categories: those over which you have 1) direct control, 2) indirect control, or 3) no control. If you determine you have no control, don't waste your time, energy or effort on that condition - it's not your problem. If you determine you have indirect control, assess what measures you can employ to influence the problem and act. If you determine the condition is a problem you can control, then deal with it. Subordinate feelings to values. Choose how you respond to circumstances. Work on your self.

Driven by Desire
Successful people are ambitious. Use your time and opportunity in this life for something worthwhile. No remedy exists for lack of ambition. Your "Definite Chief Aim," the thing you want, crave, yearn for, is the starting point of achievement. Motivation to acts springs from the strength of your desire. Cultivate desire. Focus your thoughts on what you want, and stoke the fire of desire until you generate enough heat to act. Then pour gas on the fire and accelerate. Desire fuels all achievement.

Decisive
Successful people decide. They realize a seventy percent solution put into action is better than the perfect solu-

tion never implemented. Reach decisions promptly; change decisions slowly. Overcome procrastination by deciding. Success requires no explanations; failure permits no alibis. Deeds, not words, count. Become self-determining. The world makes way for the one who knows where he or she is going.

Goal Oriented
Begin with the end in mind. All things are created twice: first mentally then physically. A definite purpose, a well defined goal (specific; with a deadline; includes the method of payment), is the first step to realizing that objective. Choose wisely. Real achievement is success with self, not things - mastery over self. Write a personal mission statement. Shift from focusing on people and things to centering on principles. Peak performers visualize and experience the objective before executing. Identify roles and goals. Without involvement, there is no commitment. Shared vision has tremendous power.

Focused
Successful people concentrate on their goals and minimize effort and energy expended on other pursuits. Keep your eye on the ball, the most important ball. Don't take on too much. Seek to focus as many thoughts, over as much time as possible, on your most important aim. Trying to do too much or too many different things will only diffuse your effort and dilute your results. Focus the irresistible force of willpower on the task at hand - that most important one thing.

Action Oriented
The only thing that stands between you and your intention is the will to act and the faith to believe. Happiness is found in doing, not merely possessing. No matter what the object of desire: riches, fame, relationships

or whatever your goal might be - in the end, your objective, and the result, are always feelings. Your journey of life is experience, is feelings. Action is what happens when thoughts and feelings gain enough energy to interact with "the world out there." Action is energized thought. People who act have focused enough energy to overcome resistance, to overcome complacency, to overcome fear. Action is energy materialized in motion. Every result is energy - action is more energy. If you want a result apply more energy - act. Successful people are action oriented. You can be too.

Putting First Things First
Goethe said, "Things that matter most must never be at the mercy of things that matter least." Focus on the important things - opportunities, not problems. Act. Exercise independent will to become principle centered. You must have a vision of the end result. Focus on your unique contribution. Organize and execute around priorities. Make and keep commitments.

Going Above and Beyond
Successful people make a habit of doing more than they are paid for. They understand doing a thing well is its own reward. Doing something well is never trouble. Rarely are the energy and effort needed to exceed expectations burdensome. The good will and gratitude you earn by doing more than what is asked, or more than what is expected, far exceeds the cost.

Planning
Successful people crystallize desire into action through organized planning. Desire is the launch pad of achievement. Ultimate faith produces ultimate results, but if you cannot act on pure faith, advance incrementally. From the desire, establish a goal, next make a plan. The plan defines a route, the resources and the allies

required to achieve the determined objective. Prepare simple, clear, and precise plans. Simplicity is essential for understanding. Planning, not the plan, is key. By planning you are focusing more thought energy on the desired result, which automatically is moving the universe to produce the desired outcome. Circumstances change the instant you begin executing a plan - be prepared to adjust.

Disciplined
Successful people maintain self-control; they are self-disciplined. Discipline is the ability to stick to a task, commit to a purpose, or adhere to a code despite the distractions, the inhibitions, or the obstacles. Disciplined people overcome resistant or distracting feelings by reinforcing specific habits that move them in the direction of the desired outcome. Success and failure are largely the result of habit. Discipline derives from discipline. Successful people make a habit of doing things failures don't like to do (strength of purpose wins). Time management is a misnomer: the key is managing your self (prioritize what's on your schedule).

Trusting
Trust is the highest form of human motivation. Successful people trust themselves, a higher power, and other people. Trust is both a conviction to an idea or ideal, and faith in other people, systems, or outcomes. Complete trust removes anxiety and allows freedom of action. Building and repairing trust in relationships is a long-term investment.

Faithful
Faith is knowing what you seek will come to pass. Visualize and believe in the attainment of your desire. You have no limits except those you acknowledge. Nurture a faithful state of mind. Build faith by inducing, creating, affirming repeatedly. Mix thoughts with emotion.

Dominating thoughts will reproduce. Write your intention down frequently. Ensure your intent conforms to laws of nature. If you intend to receive, determine what you will first give.

Self-Confident
Be secure in your ability to think, to act, to receive. Cultivate self-confidence by thinking and acting more deliberately. If large, grand or substantive results seem out of reach, undertake small and manageable tasks. Frequency substitutes for power. Reinforce gains, build on wins - success begets success. Attention, focus and practice build confidence.

Courageous
Overcome fear - observe your fear, accept the feeling and act despite it. Banish the six basic fears: poverty, criticism, ill health, loss of love of someone, old age, and death. To clear out indecision, doubt, and fear take inventory of your beliefs, predispositions, and tendencies. Fears are nothing more than states of mind. You have the ability to completely control you mind. Your thoughts are the one thing over which you have absolute control. As the mind can build or destroy, create your state of mind. Refuse to manufacture alibis and excuses. Create results.

Plato said, "The first and best victory is to conquer self." Force life to pay what is asked.

And as Napoleon Hill said, "Life is a checkerboard, the player opposite you is time. If you hesitate before moving, or neglect to move promptly, your pieces will be wiped off the board. You are playing against a partner who will not tolerate indecision."

In Control of Thought
Thoughts are things; powerful things. All achievement

springs from an idea. If you don't have the strength or the self-discipline to control or focus your thoughts for any length of time - substitute frequency for duration. By means of some reminder (a note on the mirror, in your planner, or your cell phone), set aside a moment or two to focus your thoughts. Baby step by baby step take control of your thoughts. Change your mind from failure to success consciousness.

Exercise your transmitter and receiver. Your brain is both a transmitter and a receiver of thought - a broadcasting and receiving station. Unseen and intangible forces influence the mind. Some of these influences are from other minds, some are from a more profound source. Emotions increase the vibration frequency of thought. Working in concert with other minds creates more energy to influence the unseen, intangible forces. While most people wish for treasure, having a definite plan, plus burning desire, is the truest means to realize riches.

Imaginative
Imagination is the workshop of the mind. Successful people utilize the tools at their disposal to imagine new results. Synthesize existing ideas in new ways. Foster new thoughts. Create and nurture new visions. By exercising imagination you fuel desire. Seeing the object, the outcome, clearly, in minute detail, builds faith. If you can see the goal undoubtedly in your imagination you can more exactly define your purpose. Through continued, determined effort you can increase urgency and ultimately drive action to bring your vision into reality.

Intuitive
Life is organized to grow, to expand. You are meant to succeed. Nature never deviates from established law. Don't over complicate your life by ignoring the guides

who are assisting you. Pay attention to your sixth sense: creative imagination and intuition. Emulate the great by feeling and acting. Leverage sources of inspiration. Rely on your gut and act accordingly.

Able to Influence the Subconscious

Successful people have discovered how to leverage more power by influencing forces beyond conscious thought. The subconscious is the connecting link to infinite intelligence. The subconscious can be directed only through habit. Voluntarily plant in your subconscious mind the plan, the thought, or the purpose you desire to manifest. By envisioning your desired result you deliberately influence your subconscious mind. Use repetition and the power of positive emotions (desire, faith, love, sex, enthusiasm, romance, hope) to energize your purpose.

Your subconscious responds to feelings; train your subconscious by mixing emotions and feelings with words. Here also frequency can substitute for duration - many small steps cover the same distance as a few large ones. Envision your future clearly, "as if." See yourself both achieving your objective (in real time - now) and rendering the service (payment) necessary to receive what you desire.

Masters and Employs Specialized Knowledge

In an increasingly diverse and complex world successful people must focus and specialize to master a field. Education is a means to draw knowledge and develop from within. The world is awash in knowledge, so focus on something useful. Focusing and building the required expertise takes time and effort. In round numbers: to stand amongst the best in the world at something requires on the order of five to ten years and 7,500 - 10,000 hours of deliberate practice or committed study. Once having made the commitment and paid the price, you might as well finish. You can master a very specialized field - a small niche - in a fraction of the time of a large, competitive field. Keep learning to organize and intelligently direct knowledge.

Shows Leadership

The principle asset a leader brings to any undertaking is the ability to inspire. A leader inspires through vision and motivation - the exact same attributes, by the way, necessary for individual success. Leaders provide the vision, focus and discipline to harmonize intent and focus energy to achieve more powerful, grander results. Leaders exhibit unwavering courage; self-control; a keen sense of justice; definiteness of decision; definiteness of plans; the habit of doing more than paid for; pleasing personality; sympathy and understanding; mastery of detail; cooperation and collaboration. Leaders assume full responsibility.

Loving

Love - pure love - is the ultimate value, the guiding principle, the foundational state of reality. One who loves truly always wins. Love has no preconceptions. Love has no attachments. Love embraces the outcome, accepts it, releases it and continues to grow. Perfect love is perfectly in tune with life. Love can never lose entirely - every action, every outcome is an expression of life and a steppingstone to ultimate fulfillment. Make love a verb.

Operate by the "Golden Rule"

The Golden Rule is to do unto others as you would have them do unto you. Successful people think win/win. Apply the Golden Rule in everything you do. Successful people naturally exhibit, or deliberately nurture, a pleasing personality.

Choose win/win or no deal: there is plenty for everyone. It's not your way or my way; it's a better way, a higher way. Cooperate and collaborate (don't compete) and you'll create more for everyone.

Communicators
Communication is a critical life skill. Successful people cooperate and collaborate - they do not compete (in the sense of knocking others down). To work well with others, master the skills of communication. Seek first to understand, observe, listen, grow; then seek to be understood. Listen intent to understand rather than intent to reply. See things from the other person's perspective. Construct the opposing case first. Rephrase, reflect - listen.

Builds Alliances - Teams
Successful people know everything they think and feel and do affects other people. In the same way they realize everything other people think and feel and do affects them. So they seek like-minded, positive associates who will devote time, energy and effort to coordinate and collaborate growth. Build a master mind group. A group of supportive, positive people serves as a multiplier, a driving force toward achievement. Mutually supportive alliances are powerful. Leverage the power of common intention and positive emotions. Join forces with trusted allies; ensure unity of effort, and succeed.

Seeks to Synergize
You are not on this journey alone. Achieving anything substantial requires significant energy that you can access through other people. Cooperate, collaborate, work with other people to achieve common, worthwhile ends. Synergy is the essence of principle-centered leadership. Value differences while building on strengths. Tolerate others - their purposes, their intentions, and their personalities. You can learn something

from every person you encounter. Leverage collective assets to compensate for weaknesses.

Flexible and Adaptable
Successful people are focused on results, but not attached to them. No plan is foolproof, no path set without challenges. Successful people remain flexible and adaptable in dealing with life's detours. They realize that the ultimate purpose for all activity, all manifestation is growth, is experience, is becoming, so they remain flexible and adaptable both on the journey and upon arriving at the temporary destination. In warfare it's said, "the enemy has a vote," so it is in life. It is not so much an external enemy that is your concern; rather, you must overcome your self. You must adjust to new circumstances, modify your attempts, and fine-tune your actions to keep moving in the right direction. There is no other way to succeed.

Periodically Renew
Everyone needs to rest, recover and renew their body, their mind, and their spirit. Achieving a balance between the energy you absorb and energy you expend is essential for continued peak performance. Strike and maintain a healthy equilibrium in all areas of life: physical (fit and healthy); mental (sharp, inquisitive and growing); social (vibrantly connected with others); and spiritual (nurture your connection with the greater reality and expand your perspective). Create an upward spiral of progress from the inside out.

Conform to the Law of Life
Successful people act in accordance with the law of nature and the law of life: effort begets reward. Effort is required before reward is received. To get one must give. This is a law of economics and a law of life. Every person has the opportunity to render useful service and

to collect riches in proportion to the value of that service. Other people can invest for you. The results they produce will enliven and enrich your environment, but in order for you to grow, to flourish, to become you must put forth effort yourself. Every "thing" that manifests in life, all circumstances, all experiences are mergers of, are expressions of energy. You must invest, focus, employ energy to enjoy, experience, or realize an outcome that allows you to grow. Realize you must give first before you can receive.

Persistent
Sustain the effort necessary to induce faith. If you can't cultivate faith in your mind, act "as if" repeatedly. Persist in action. If you intently desire something, fuel your desire and persist. Obstacles and failings are tests. You only truly fail if you quit. Look at a "failure" as an opportunity to learn and grow and reorient. If you want to achieve more, sooner, fail faster. Train yourself to persist despite obstacles. Define your purpose. Construct a definite plan (even if the plan only consists of the next step). Maintain your mental focus. Build a friendly and supportive alliance. Pray and persist.

Inspiring
Upon finding their way, successful people find their voice. They then use that voice to move themselves to success and inspire others to find their way. In this age of knowledge workers, we are interconnected by reinforcing systems. It's easy for people to be absorbed by the size, scope and power of the systems. Every life is a journey to fulfillment. Every person has vast potential to be and become. Seek to move to greatness. Live a full and fulfilling life. Execute, act with passion. Put forth a significant contribution. Help others through your thoughts, your words, and by your example.

• • • • • • •

This list of attributes is not to suggest you have to build a perfect person or a perfect life by mastering each component. Someone who ultimately aligns their life with a higher purpose and conforms to laws of life naturally exhibits these traits. If you do not place yourself in the same category as the successful people, then learn new skills until you can change your belief.

When someone first learns to juggle, they don't begin with three, or four, or five balls. They begin with one. Don't attempt to juggle all the balls; start with one. Select one attribute. Start with one you can internalize and embrace. Work on that one, and gradually as your skills improve, add more. You see, what you are really working on is your faith. You are overcoming fear one step at a time. As you take small steps on a long and fulfilling journey you gain confidence and you build faith. You can be and become all you are destined to be.

The only obstacle you must overcome is your internal resistance. Let go. It will be okay. If you really want to accelerate your progress, then focus on the most important thing.

THE SINGLE MOST IMPORTANT THING

What is it you intend to achieve?

You see it doesn't matter where you are in the pack - whether you are the leader or at the tail end. It doesn't matter how fast you are going or who you are competing against. It doesn't matter what kind of baggage you are carrying or what you've overcome to get where you are. The only thing that matters now is where you are headed.

You are GUARANTEED TO SUCCEED! No question, no excuses, no doubt. You will absolutely succeed in this life. You will get everything you claim.

The question is not, Will you succeed? The question is, What will you succeed at?

What will you claim?

Your goal - your objective - your aim is the most important thing.

Life is moving. Even if you don't want to move, life will move you. You have to choose your direction. You choose what you are aiming for. Make it something worthwhile; something deserving of your life, your energy, your focus.

Life is either a playground or a battlefield - a condition you, in your mind's eye determine. While the rules are set, the options vary. The buffet of life offers a multitude of choices - some healthy, some forgiving, and some downright dangerous. You get to choose.

Life, however, has an intention. Life's purpose, life's motive, life's aim is to expand - to grow. As an element of a majestic landscape, a flourishing tapestry, an unfolding drama, you have a role to perform. Your purpose is to grow - to add life - to increase value. How you contribute is not defined, but that you contribute is mandatory.

All we know of life is in motion. Every component of matter and energy, substance and awareness is changing, expanding, increasing in complexity and beauty. The note you play in the grand symphony adds to the work's texture, depth, diversity. Choose your note carefully.

Your intention is the most important thing.

Your life, this world, this reality is in constant flux. Life is change. Your gift, your treasure, is to experience the magnificence, the splendor, the glory of it all. The price for admission is to make a deposit. You must contribute.

Life is moving in a direction. The forces of history are amassing. The story is building toward a crescendo.

The divine will is revealing its nature and its endless compassion in a tale beyond human comprehension. The secret to successfully navigating your course, to completing your journey, is to advance correctly. The secret of success is to move in the right direction.

Make no mistake about it - to be alive is to be moving. You cannot stay still. You are either increasing or diminishing, growing or dying. Don't head in the wrong direction. Don't work against life. Don't resist the forces that beckon you to grow, to be, to become. These forces are working for your good, for our good, for the greater good.

You have chosen to live, to journey in this time and in this place. Moving is not an option. Moving toward something worthwhile, something fulfilling is your choice.

A law of this existence, a rule of this game is that you move toward what you focus your thoughts on. And, what you focus your thoughts on moves toward you. Focus your thoughts wisely. You will assuredly hit what you aim at. You are guaranteed to succeed in reaching your objective. Knowing you can't miss, choose a goal that is worth the effort. Choose a purpose and a destination that measure up to the divine promise and brilliant potential you possess.

For your intention, your goal, your purpose is the most important thing.

Invest your time and your energy - your thoughts, your words, and your actions - on the most important thing.

What do you want to achieve?
What do you want to do?
What do you want to become?
How do you want to feel?
Focus on the most important thing.

5
HOW LIFE WORKS

Picture yourself comfortably reclining in a first-class seat of an airliner. You have as your goal to travel to some exotic location for the vacation of a lifetime. You are relaxed, carefree, and happy. An undercurrent of excitement courses through your body. You anticipate sun and fun, laughs and adventure - the time of your life. Your entire trip has been effortless and trouble free. You are on your way, and sure to arrive soon.

At any point along the way, from the beginning of your journey to your arrival at your exotic destination, have you needed to know how the transportation functions? Do you need to know how the car works in order to drive it? Do you need to know how the train functions to board it? Do you need to know how the plane stays aloft to fly in it?

You don't need to know how all the vehicles that transport you work. You only need enough knowledge to connect with the vehicle in a way that moves you toward your objective. You only need to have enough faith and courage and motivation to use the transportation. You don't need to know how things work to move you forward; you just need to accept that they work.

So it is with life. Life works when you do. You don't need to know *how* life works, just that life *does* work. The challenge is that cooperating with life requires a degree of faith, a degree of courage, and a degree of motivation. The degree you embody and exhibit each of these traits determines the degree to which life works.

You will see "The Success Spectrum" illustrated in an earlier chapter once again later in this book. This continuum represents measures and degrees of success. Taken as a whole the spectrum attempts to represent the opportunities inherent in life. At one end of the scale is very limited opportunity, while at the other end is infinite possibility. The real kicker is that we, you, and I, and every other person on the planet, get to choose where on the continuum we live our lives - perspective and focus determine experience.

While certain factors are the primary considerations for success in life (moving in the right direction, overcoming ego) three aspects of character matter most: faith, courage, and motivation.

Notice, like with the exciting vacation travel, success in life doesn't hinge on knowing how life works. Success in life hinges on: 1. Your faith in what life will bring - that is, your beliefs and expectations about life; 2. Your courage and willingness to advance on faith; and 3. Your motivation, which is the energy of desire applied to realizing your objectives.

Most people, early in life, develop a tendency to fear. Since you are reading this you (like me) are probably stuck doing battle with ego. Fear is a constant companion. Fear, being the social fellow that it is, invites doubt and opens the door to judgment, blame, and a willingness to play victim. If you're not careful you could quickly slide into a party of despair. The key to success in the journey of life is changing your mindset from fear to faith.

It's time we set upon a new course.

To begin to get the upper hand with ego, we've got to release ego's grip. A strategy ego frequently employs is to demand to know how something will unfold before ego permits action. If ego has hold, by figuring out how life works we can start turning in a new direction and get moving. You overcome fear by action. You succeed in life by acting. If the impediment to action is ego's need to know how - let's get past this hurdle. That is why we are here, exploring this subject now.

The intent is to reduce the influence of ego by understanding how life works. We don't need to know every detail of how; we just need to move from fear to faith. But by knowing more about how life works we will broaden our perspectives and discover more opportunities. This should prove to be a useful diversion to set things right.

SEEKING ANSWERS

People, as a way of understanding the environment and happenings of this world, need to break big concepts and complex happenings into small, manageable pieces. By examining the pieces we hope to identify causes, recognize patterns, and ultimately ascribe meaning.

Some people accept the view that there are some things beyond knowing. Some things are just beyond the human intellect's ability to comprehend. Other people, however, are convinced, though we may not know everything yet, human beings will someday uncover the mysteries of the universe. We will come to know all there is to know and understand all that can be known.

Which side of this debate are you on?

As for knowledge and a human being's ability to understand, I think we have the deck stacked against us.

We live a physical life, in a physical universe - a limited existence. Though we don't know how, or what, or why, something does exist beyond. Something is capable of bridging the gap between the physical universe and that something else - whether you call it a void, another dimension (or perhaps multiple dimensions), or a spiritual realm.

You've seen illustrations depicting the aspects of a human being. The drawings are usually intended to distinguish component parts of the whole. Here is a depiction that I find valuable.

At the center of this diagram is "body." That the body exists is an aspect of self that will elicit universal acceptance. Everyone believes in the body because everyone possesses a body. The body operates on the physical dimension of reality. The body relies on the five senses and the functioning of mind, to survive and thrive.

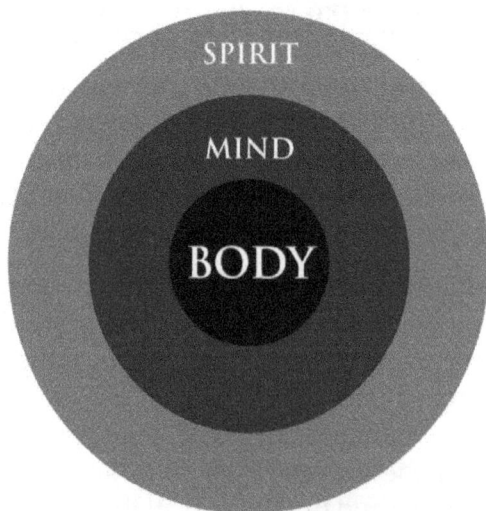

DIMENSIONS OF BEING (NARROW)

Once we move from body to mind, however, agreement is more difficult to discern. For our purposes here suffice it to say, the mind is more capable than the body. At the bare minimum the mind (in the most physical terms - the brain) manages the systems of the body. The mind receives and interprets environmental stimuli. And, most importantly, the mind determines action.

Moving up one step (and venturing into territory virtually uncharted and therefore prone to disagreement) is spirit. Spirit is the realm of the undefined. The energy and substance of spirit are immaterial. Time, the boundary and connections between these, and aspects of these dimensions all may be incredibly different from what body and mind observe and understand. Spirit is the realm of faith. Though not demonstrated in the graphic, spirit has an exponentially larger perspective.

A human being is a complex entity, operating in a complex environment. The truth is, though we attempt to isolate and address some single aspect of the whole, the whole is always interconnected.

This journey into knowing how will bear fruit, but it won't be completely satisfying. Something beyond our capacity to know exists. Whether or not we can sort that out, for the time being, you and I have more practical concerns. We have the opportunity of a lifetime. We are here now, living, breathing, experiencing. Our task is to make this journey as worthwhile and fulfilling as we possibly can. We are launching into the task of breaking down the whole.

DIFFERENT PERSPECTIVES ON THE SAME TRUTH

Theologians, philosophers, and scientists are not all that different from one another. They all seek to understand the world and humanity's place in it. All three recognize the universe is in motion. They accept, to varying degrees, we don't understand everything. They realize each life is temporary. They just operate from different motives.

Theologians attempt to understand the cosmos and mankind's place in creation relative to an ultimate being with an ultimate motive. Theologians seek to determine the implications of a temporary existence in a constantly changing reality relative to an infinite, timeless and immortal reality. Deliverance from this reality - salvation - is their theme.

Philosophers attempt a more practical inquiry into the cosmos and mankind's place in it. Philosophers operate comfortably in that space between known (verifiable - i.e. scientific) reality and the unexplained and potentially unknowable. Philosophers seek wisdom. In wisdom they identify truth about this reality. They then can apply the truths they identify to help people live full and fulfilling lives.

Scientists attempt the most practical inquiry of all into the cosmos and mankind's place in it. They ignore the unknown and potentially unknowable and focus on the observable and measurable components of reality. Through their research and inquiry they seek to find how life functions. From these observations people can then learn to manipulate reality to advantage. Science may never answer the big questions, but science does facilitate the increasingly productive manipulation of energy and matter.

Science bridges the mystery of energy and the reality of action. Those who deny the power of thought find relief in the practical application of action. Scientists have developed an intentional process to observe, measure and assess the physical world. We can use this method to advance our inquiry.

THE SCIENTIFIC METHOD

The scientific method is a way of exploring the physical universe.

The process amounts to a body of techniques for investigating natural phenomena to acquire new knowledge, or to correct and integrate previous knowledge.

The scientific method is a deliberate, systematic approach to the exploration of the physical universe. To be considered "scientific" an inquiry must gather empirical (observable, repeatable) and measurable data and conform to specific principles of reasoning. The method defines a way of asking and answering questions by observing and testing physical reality.

The steps of the scientific method are:

- Ask a question
- Conduct background research
- Propose a hypothesis
- Test the hypothesis (experiment)
- Analyze data and draw a conclusion
- Communicate results

Hypotheses are explanations of phenomena. A researcher designs studies or experiments controlling variables and purposefully testing hypotheses. The intent is to measure, control and document every input so that the steps of an experiment can be repeated and results duplicated.

A defining feature of the scientific method is that, in theory, adherents attempt to remain as objective as possible and let reality speak for itself. Unbiased results, even results that contradict accepted theories, are intended and welcome.

While science evolved from theological and philosophical inquiry, scientists have carved out a realm of exploration distinct from theologians and philosophers. Where theology and philosophy venture into realms of pure theory, speculation and faith, scientists restrict their inquiries to measurable, observable phenomena.

While theologians and philosophers contribute immeasurably to our understanding of what is and what we know, scientists focus on practical applications in the physical world. Through deliberate inquiry and experimental verification, science has moved humanity from the stone age to the information age. Sometimes by great leaps and bounds, but more frequently by disciplined observation and incremental improvement.

The science of success is broad and deep. There exist, however, a few nuggets of knowledge that prove to be the keys to operating most productively in this reality.

WHAT DO WE KNOW?

What would you consider as an absolute? That is what we identify and know as the foundation elements of experience. You might automatically think: death and taxes - those are absolutes. Consider for a moment something more fundamental.

Everything "out there," everything we experience with our senses, is energy. Energy is an absolute. The universe, our solar system, this planet, and your body are composed of energy. Organized energy we most frequently refer to as matter, but nonetheless it is energy.

We used to think atoms were the smallest element of matter - organized energy. Atoms were combinations of protons, neutrons, and electrons maintaining a delicate connection and balance. But as scientists' capability improved (instruments as well as theory) they discovered that components exist that are smaller than what had been identified as atoms. An entirely new language has evolved to label and describe these tiny subatomic particles. Leptons, quarks, and neutrinos have all entered the scientific lexicon.

Scientists have struggled to isolate and identify the smallest component of matter. The discovery has most investigators perplexed. Trying to decode the building blocks of matter, scientists have found space - and something else. That something else is difficult, at best, to isolate. As scientists have tried to observe the smallest particle it disappears then reappears somewhere else. They have surmised but not settled that the smallest element of matter is both a wave of energy and a particle. The element actually transitions between both states.

Everything we observe is energy in some form.

As we live in a dualistic reality, that is, everything has its contrary; every force has an equal and opposite force. So too energy has need of one other constituent to exist: awareness. Energy is everything out there. Awareness is recognizing there exists an "out there." Science, philosophy and religion have not settled the question of whether reality exists out there or whether reality is a projection of mind. Are we really engaged in a physical reality or is it all illusion? Are we alive in a tangible world or are we dreaming an elaborate dream? In practical terms, it doesn't matter.

We are left navigating this reality. And, this reality - life - conforms to certain patterns of functioning. The systems of this world, this solar system, galaxy, and known universe operate in distinct, definable ways. The universe - life - adheres to what we describe as laws.

REALITY CONFORMS
TO CERTAIN LAWS

The simplest, and probably most used illustration of a "law of nature" or "scientific law" is gravity. Everyone, and every "thing" on earth conforms to the law of gravity. Everything that has mass is attracted to everything else that has mass. The earth itself exerts a force on all things. No one can ignore the force. People cannot determine they don't believe in gravity and therefore escape the force gravity exerts. People who have never even heard of the term gravity must still adhere to its affects. Everyone on earth must deal with gravity, whether they want to or not.

Though we might complain from time to time about the existence of gravity (like when the bathroom scale offers its reading), it is a force we cannot ignore. We must conform to the influence of gravity. The oceans move rhythmically and surely conforming to the gravitational pull between the earth and the moon. Gravity is a force of nature. Gravity is so pervasive, so predictable, and so reliable that we call it a law. And everyone obeys this law.

Success 101: How Life Works

The pantheon of scientific laws addresses such areas as gravity, motion, energy transfer in thermodynamics and heat, electromagnetism, and so on. Though scientists and philosophers argue over the details, people conform to the laws and to the realities the world presents.

Many inventors use the laws to their advantage. They invent devices or processes that leverage known laws to solve problems. Complying with the law has its benefits.

Though not considered "laws," as these don't apply to all known systems, we recognize and adhere to a host of other boundaries and patterns in life. We have simple physical limitations defined by our stature and strength. We grow and age at a pace normally outside our control. We have a specific limit of time on this earth; birth marks the beginning and death marks the end. We possess certain attributes, skills and capabilities. Most people do not even begin to tap the vast potential they possess, but even unhampered we have limitations. We need air, food, and water to survive. If we get too cold or too hot we die. We cannot fly through the air or live under water without the aid of mechanical devices. We possess a certain degree of muscular strength and intellectual acuity. As social beings we can clearly leverage the talents, strength and efforts of other people. But, even together, in groups we have limitations.

The systems of our world operate in defined cycles. The rotation of the earth results in light and darkness. The orbit of the earth around the sun drives the rhythm of seasons. Energy from the sun sustains and impacts life on earth at all times. Even the interplay of the planets has an effect on the beings here on earth.

All life operates within cycles of growth, maturity, decline, and transition. This is a reality we cannot escape. Everything begins, grows, and decays in ever renewing cycles. To be alive is to be codependent. We survive as part of biological and mechanical systems. Oxygen, nutrition, and other energy transference processes sustain life. If we sever our ties with any of these systems we die.

The physical world operates by mechanical laws. Some laws, however, people routinely attempt to ignore. These laws of nature though, are self-enforcing. The laws of life, the "rules of the game," are the way things work. You don't have a choice about whether to comply. You ignore laws of life at your own peril.

Our universe functions a certain way. It's just the way things are.

People, however, expend an exorbitant amount of energy attempting to evade the law. Ever in search of a shortcut, people chase after what appears to be an exception to the rule, only to find the law stands firm. Amongst the rules of life we most often and most painfully attempt to ignore:

1) Life intends to grow.

2) Thoughts becomes things.

3) You receive in proportion to what you give.

Life is an ever-expanding proposition. Your reason for being, your purpose in life is to grow, to become, to contribute. You are meant to add value. Resisting growth, failing to move forward, destroying instead of building are futile. The law of life requires growth. Choosing not to comply means ultimately being swept aside.

Thought is energy, a powerful, creative form of energy. Within the mind resides the power to create the circumstances and experiences of life. Through the power of thought, the things people think about begin to take shape. If you focus thought, the experience you cultivate manifests.

Most people, unaware of this reality or unwilling to put forth effort, refuse to discipline thought.

People avoid thinking. Evidence of this abounds. Look around.

And finally, people constantly lament their state of lack. They fail to understand that a person receives in proportion to the value they create. You cannot reap what you have not sown.

Reward is proportionate to contribution. Mistakenly having bought into the notion that fulfillment is found in stuff, in consuming, we seek first to receive. The law is this: one must contribute before one takes; one must give before one receives. It takes effort before one experiences reward. Any other choice is an attempt to break the law – but it is a law that can't be broken.

Life is a constant struggle for those who disregard the law. It need not be so difficult.

Living is a measure of complying with the rules of the game and the laws of life. Don't ignore the most basic and powerful laws. Grow by focusing your thoughts and taking action to add value. Once you contribute, you receive what you are due.

The laws of life do not discriminate; they work for everyone. Laws offer the opportunity to flourish, to excel, to enjoy a full and fulfilling life. Attempting to not comply invites pain-filled consequences. Don't ignore the laws; live by them.

THE SCIENCE OF PRODUCING

What we know about life is that all that is out there is energy. Matter is organized energy.

The experience of life is the translation of external energy into internal feelings. The life and times of being is manipulating energy to accomplish everything required to survive, to grow, and to flourish. We live in a cause and effect existence. Everything, invariably, resonates from and originates in a cause.

Because of the complexity of life, sometimes identifying a cause can be problematic. Scientists have run models attempting to explain a series of causes from observable effects. The scientists have, in theory, returned to the moment of the "big bang" - the birth of the known universe - but then they are stuck. Working purely in the mechanical dimension seems insufficient. When you arrive at the beginning, then where do you go for cause?

In our physical reality we constantly, deliberately, and frequently mistakenly manipulate energy to produce results. Everything is in motion. Cause and effect are working - creating, arriving, recombining. As we use energy we contribute to this process. Often without knowing or consciously intending we move energy - we cause effects.

Let's take a look at the science of manipulating energy. We have determined everything is energy. Energy in flux, in motion, produces results. The interplay of energy causes effects.

First we must agree on the definition of some terms: energy, force, mass, acceleration, work, and power. Don't worry about mastering the fine distinctions of these definitions, as the result will be quite clear, regardless of the nuances.

Energy: undefined.

We simply don't know what energy is. It is the Mysterious Everything. Ultimately energy is the formless substance of the universe. It is the dynamic quality of what is.

Theologians and philosophers explore and debate the nature and origin of energy. Scientists and engineers study how energy behaves and through devices and processes use that knowledge to rearrange and manipulate reality.

Scientists have settled on energy as an abstract concept to describe changes they observe in the physical world. One of the simplest and best definitions of energy (related to the physical definition below) is: the property, or characteristic, of stuff that makes things happen.

The universe, as we know it, is made up of stuff. The smallest observable and theoretical parts of known reality consist of waves and particles with attractive and repulsive properties. The universe consists of something (or you might conceptualize "things") that moves, something that changes, something with the capacity to combine, dissolve, form and reform.

For the route we are traversing, however, the following meaning may help:

> Physics definition of *energy*: the capacity of a physical system to do work.

Matter: organized energy. Energy arranged in such a way as to have a definable, observable mass. Matter is often considered equivalent or synonymous to energy.

Object: entity of matter; a defined collection of energy.

Mass: the measure of an object's resistance to the change of its speed.

In common usage mass is often equated to weight; however, weight considers an object's resistance to gravity. Mass, in scientific usage, applies to a broader array of forces than just gravity. An object's mass is the same regardless of environment. Mass is akin to an object's potential energy - if energy (or matter) is taken away, an object's mass is less; if energy (or matter) is added, an object's mass increases.

Acceleration: the rate at which an object changes velocity.

The nuance with acceleration is that it means a measure of the change of an object's speed. That is the increasing speed (faster) of an object. To accelerate an object changes position relative to its start point at an increasing rate.

Force: an influence causing an object to change speed, direction, or shape.

The only "substance" we can identify, though we cannot accurately define it, is energy. So to better understand an "influence," we circle back and arrive at energy. Any form of influence is energy. Energy applied in a given way is force, an influence to change some "thing."

In scientific parlance:

Force = Mass x Acceleration

The amount of force is described as the potential energy of an object (mass) relative to the object's rate of change.

Work: the product of force through the distance over which it acts.

We commonly consider work as physical or mental effort directed toward the production or accomplishment of something. A strict definition, but one related to what we commonly call work, is force applied to an object over a distance.

As represented in physics:

Work = Force x Distance

Power: the rate at which energy is transferred, used, or transformed.

Energy transfer can be used to do work, so power can be understood as the rate at which work is performed.

Power = Work / Time

I've taken you through these definitions to arrive at two amazing, incredible, and for many people, unbelievable truths:

1. THOUGHT IS ENERGY

We have determined in the big scheme of things, human beings don't know much. We can't define energy - we just don't know what it is - and we don't understand awareness or consciousness.

Rather than do nothing from ignorance, we do the best we can with what we have. Though we don't know what the building blocks of the universe are, we can in fact observe what is, measure it, and seek to understand its properties. By so doing we can manipulate stuff to meet our needs and advance our purposes.

If we label everything as energy (other people choose to label that "mysterious everything" as God or love or universe), then thought also is a form of energy.

Conventional wisdom asserts that if you want to achieve success you must WORK HARD. To accomplish any worthwhile task an individual must apply his or her assets (intellect, energy, talents, etc.) over a period of time toward achieving a specific end.

To produce any result an individual applies power. He or she works over a period of time, exerting a force (influence) in a given direction to manifest a specific result.

Working back through our sequence of scientific equations we realize, to accomplish anything requires force (consisting of the mysterious everything) directed toward, ultimately, matter (more of the mysterious everything).

Through the application of force, human beings insert themselves in - are part of - the physical system of the universe to become CAUSE. Through thought people cause things to happen, things to manifest - people create. Cause automatically and always produces EFFECT.

Through the energy they apply, human beings influence stuff and create things. That energy, the initiating point for human being's engagement with or navigation through the physical universe, is THOUGHT.

Thought is energy. Thought is a force. Thought influences and acts on the mysterious everything. Thought is a cause. And thought always produces an effect.

Thoughts literally become things.

Thoughts are creative energy.

A human being can and does influence the universe, the world, and the circumstances he or she experiences by way of the thoughts he or she entertains.

As mentioned before, researchers have determined each of us experiences or entertains between 20,000 and 60,000 thoughts per day. Each and every day, seven days per week, 52 weeks per year we have at our disposal a constantly renewing supply of creative energy. Every thought absolutely and unfailingly influences the mysterious everything. Every thought moves the universe. Every thought creates something. Every thought is connected to something else.

But not every thought is powerful enough to manifest in totality. Not every thought results in an experience - an object, a condition, or a circumstance. Most thoughts are fleeting and underpowered. Their influence is temporary and minimal. While most impulses of thought flitter away as seemingly imperceptibly as they came, every thought contributes to the effects you experience.

Everything is energy.

If you want to build a house, you can calculate the amount of resources and labor required to complete the project. You'll need lumber and cement, nails and shingles, wiring and plumbing, paint and power, and numerous other resources to build a house. You'll need the time, energy and talents of people to complete a series of complex tasks.

Building a house requires energy. Each component, every contributing element ultimately is the contribution of - that is, originates in - thought. All of the resources come available because of the thoughts of suppliers and manufacturers and distributors. The craftsmen and laborers work for various motivations, but ultimately they work because of an impulse of thought. A house, every house, is literally constructed from thought. It is initially an "idea" or "concept" in mind, and then it becomes a physical reality (it manifests) through the energy of ideas put into action.

Any effect is really a product of cause. The bigger, the grander, or the speedier the effect, the greater or more powerful the cause. Big, physical projects require significant amounts of energy. This translates into requiring considerable thought energy to build anything substantial or realize any significant result. A single, fleeting thought has energy and it automatically influences the mysterious everything, but not much. Producing specific results - effects that manifest in the physical world - requires more thought energy.

The good news is, every human being gets an endless supply of creative energy. Every day your supply of creative energy - in the form of thought - is renewed. You and every other person on the face of the earth are equal in only two measures: you have the same amount of time each day (24 hours, 1,440 hours, or 86,400 seconds). No one gets more time, no one gets less. And, thought energy. You get a fresh opportunity to create each and every day.

You are a creative being. Through your thoughts you contribute to creation. Through your thoughts you create your own story, your own epic, or your own tragedy. Your thoughts are the one thing you control and the only thing you need to control.

You absolutely and undoubtedly create each and every moment. You assuredly succeed in creating the circumstances of your life. You are guaranteed to succeed. You have all the assets, all the resources, all the power, to have, to do, to become.

The million-dollar question is not: Will I succeed? It is: What will I succeed at?

You will create something. You are creating something. Every thought that passes through your mind influences reality in countless ways.

How are you using the assets you have?

Are you focusing your assets? Are you applying them toward some worthwhile end?

Are you investing your assets to produce results you desire?

Or are you squandering your assets? Are you letting your thoughts run wild?

Is your mind, your power, your thoughts, given over to the control of other people, the media, circumstances?

If your attention is never focused, if you respond and react instead of deliberately creating, you are forfeiting your power. You are wasting your assets. You are squandering your thoughts.

Scientific law, the law of nature, asserts that causes produce effects. Force applied in a certain direction over a given distance produces specific, identifiable results. Thought is your creative form of energy. You experience the result of your thoughts every day. If you don't like the circumstances you find yourself in now, recognize that those circumstances are the result of past thoughts. If you want to produce some other result; if you want to generate some other effect; if you want to achieve something in your life - start using your thoughts. Thought is the only asset you have and the only asset you need. All creation responds to thought.

The science, the philosophy, the theology behind this truth is unmistakable and undeniable. Thoughts become things.

You just must determine what it is you want, and then apply the appropriate amount of energy to create that thing. More cause, more energy produces a bigger effect - a more substantial result. If you want to achieve or realize a different, more prosperous, more joyous, more exhilarating experience, all you have to do is think it into reality. Since thought is an energy source, and effort always precedes results, to produce anything apply the appropriate energy required.

The energy of thought increases or is empowered through a progression: thought in mind (impulse); entertain the thought (hold in mind); focus the thought; thought energized to words (or some means of communication); thought energized into action. Action is just empowered thought. Action is thought with enough energy to move in physical space over time.

Anything that you want to create is a factor of only two things: amount of energy and speed of application. To manifest or create a thing or a new reality is a matter of applying enough energy to create that thing or reality.

Perfect faith is the use of perfectly focused thought energy to create instantaneously, completely, and immediately. However, most (and by most I mean 99.99999% of people) possess nothing close to perfect faith. So, the creative process requires either more time or the contribution of more thoughts from other people.

Leaders focus thought on a given objective. Through the efforts of leaders (inspiration and motivation), people come together and apply the assets they have (originating in thought) and achieve collective results. People working together can focus immense amounts of energy toward very specific ends. This is the legacy of human achievement.

For you to achieve anything in life, you must first determine what you want, and then apply the energy necessary to realize that thing. You have the energy of twenty to sixty thousand thoughts per day to apply toward your objective. Holding the specific thought or goal in mind, focuses and applies more energy to forming that thing.

Sticking with our scientific formulas, you can look at creation this way:

Goal = TEU

Any goal, objective, aim, result, or effect equals THOUGHT ENERGY UNITS (TEU) applied.

Every thing is energy. The motion of all things in the universe produce results, results which human beings experience. Human beings contribute to the "dance of energy" by creating. We create through thought. Every result is energy. Every effect is an amount of energy. To create an effect; to bring about a result; to experience select circumstances you must apply the appropriate amount of energy. It is as simple as that.

Now remember, every thought creates. Positive thoughts produce positive results, while negative thoughts produce negative results.

Most people are undisciplined and unknowledgeable when it comes to thought. They don't even realize they have the controls. So instead of going somewhere specific, somewhere worthwhile, most people are buffeted around by circumstance. Unable to control their minds - their thoughts - people create all kinds of chaos. Much of it they regret, because their thoughts are not in concert with the main aim of life: to grow.

By squandering thoughts people unwittingly resist the advance of life. They resist opportunities to grow, opportunities to create, and opportunities to become. Instead of investing their thoughts or focusing them, they gamble them away. Each daily resupply is wasted like every other. They just as surely create results, but instead of enjoyable life experiences the results are challenging life lessons. The life lessons point back toward the truth. But the resistor persists.

Every result is the effect of a cause. The greater the effect, the more powerful the cause. Any result is guaranteed if enough thought energy is applied. For you to change your life, you must gain control of your thoughts. You must begin to deliberately apply the assets you have been squandering to produce worthwhile results.

If you move in the right direction you are a success.

2. LAW OF ATTRACTION

The second unbelievable truth is that whatever you conceive of, whatever you decide you want, wants you to the same degree.

You attract into your life whatever you desire.

You remember in our brush over particle physics we determined that in smallest measure elements are waves or particles with charges. The charges of particles either repel or attract. The law of attraction is an irrefutable process of nature where like energy attracts like energy. The charge of particles exactly match each other. What you conceive of is created in formless substance. As you focus on it and begin to move toward it, it begins to move toward you.

Think of the law of attraction as an image in a mirror. First you must see the image. The image in a mirror is a reflection of the light energy emanating from the object. In this case, let's make the object you.

You are looking at a reflection of yourself in a mirror. Consider that image the fullest and best expression of the person you yearn to become and know you can be. That person is beautiful and confident, capable and strong, prosperous and joyful. That person you see in the mirror is the ideal you. The person you know, in your heart, you are destined to be.

Now move closer to the mirror. You have physically closed the distance between you and the mirror. What happens to the image - the reflection of the ideal you?

That image is attracted to you. As you move closer to the image, the image got larger - the ideal you moved closer to you. The ideal you - that exceptional person you see in the mirror - wants you to the same degree you desire the ideal you.

Like with all energy, we can only speculate on the source of thought. Where does thought impulse come from? We know life seeks to expand, seeks to grow. We are experiencing a journey of growth, expansion. We are being and becoming. The thought-generated impulses of desire originate from the same source as the mysterious everything. Desires attract.

Desires start the process of energy moving. Desire is the starting point of all achievement. To achieve anything requires focusing the necessary amount of energy to produce the intended result. Cause always precedes effect. Desire always precedes creation.

Knowing the distance to any result is really cut in half by the law of attraction should fuel your resolve. Anything you can desire, anything you can want (if it conforms to the rules of this reality: well-being and growth) you can experience.

You are absolutely and always creating. The results you produce are either in concert with the demands of life (they conform to the law) or they resist life. When you resist you bring into your experience opportunities to learn, grow and choose again.

What you experience in life is a scientific outcome. Focus your thoughts, focus the appropriate amount of energy, and you get a specific result.

Choose wisely.

ASK, FIND WHAT WORKS, DO WHAT WORKS, REPEAT

We began our discussion here by introducing the scientific method. This is the process by which we observe, measure and learn about the physical reality we experience. The beauty of the scientific method is that it relies on the laws, the constant functioning of the universe. Given the same objects and the same conditions, anyone can and will produce the same results. Employing the scientific method is a means of proving to yourself the veracity of the claims made here.

You must first focus on something. If you want to run a test, ask a question. Duplicate the conditions that produced the result for someone else. In other words, find out what works. Once you find what works, do that thing, that process over and over again.

The world is not prejudiced. The world operates by certain principles and processes. If you want to do something, have something, or become something, find out what others did to achieve those results. Undoubtedly they focused their thoughts and applied the energy necessary to produce the results. Every creation comes into being the same way. Every circumstance is the confluence of creative energy. The more focus, the more energy applied (individually or collectively), the grander and the faster the result.

All things are possible to the one who believes. Belief is energy applied in a very specific way.

Believe and achieve.

We have taken a very brief jaunt into the world of scientific discovery. While we can understand and rationalize perspectives ranging from mechanical to quantum, we are still left with a mystery. Regardless of how all the details come together - how life works – remember that life works when you do. Some things we just don't know. Some things we are not meant to know. Accept life for what it is.

Here again is a depiction of the aspects of the human condition, somewhat expanded.

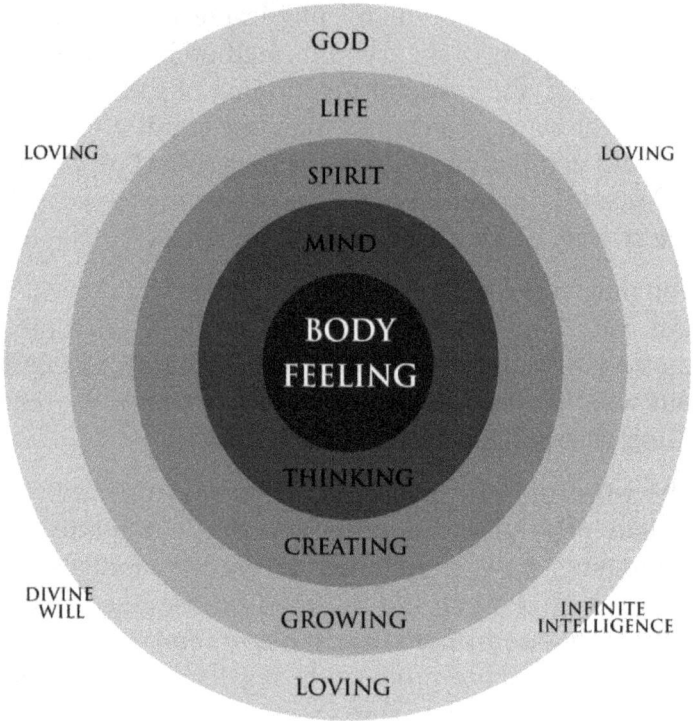

GOD

LIFE

LOVING   LOVING

SPIRIT

MIND

**BODY
FEELING**

THINKING

CREATING

DIVINE
WILL
                                    INFINITE
GROWING   INTELLIGENCE

LOVING

Dimensions Of Being (Broad)

You'll notice two additional layers.

Realize that despite all the struggles we endure in body and mind while we attempt to live in spirit - life has it under control. The big picture is beyond our knowing. Life is moving you and me, and everyone else. Act on faith. Live in faith. Trust that all is well in hand.

For us human beings, living a physical existence and traveling a dusty road, thought is the seed of all action. Thought is the energy of creation. Thought is the means by which the substance of the universe transforms into material experience. Religion, philosophy and science agree. Cause creates effects. So, choose the effect and apply the right cause. Then repeat and repeat and repeat.

Do what you can do. Live in faith. Love with all your heart.

Choose.

If you choose correctly you are destined for a spectacular life - GUARANTEED!

Success 101: How Life Works

6

CUT TO THE CHASE

A Road Map to Move from Fear to Faith, from Failure to Success

Up until now we have been focusing on the essential elements of success. These elements are components of you. They are interior work. We've discussed and considered what success means. We have revealed, uncovered, exposed, the secret of success. We have examined the one obstacle that stands in the way of achieving ultimate success. We have focused on the most important thing - that single act that determines the direction of your life. In short we have reflected upon and thought about how life works.

You may be saying: this is all well and good, but cut to the chase. What specifically can I do, *at this moment*, to change my mind, my choices, and my life?

Follow this path...

Objective: To Become Successful.

Success: Moving In The Right Direction (Action leading to Growth).

The Most Important Thing: Aim / Intention / Purpose / Focus.

Motivation: Desire.

Thoughts fueled by desire (motivation) make it happen (whatever "it" should be). Focus your thoughts on your primary aim and keep moving forward (take action).

How do you know you are moving in the right direction? Action indicates movement (making things happen - not just responding to what happens); feelings serve as your guide. Good feelings mean you are heading in the right direction. Bad feelings mean you are not.

Action is movement; feelings and intuition are your guides. Does what you are doing feel right? If so keep going; if not - change direction. To overcome the inertia of inaction or resistance of fear, start small. Do what you can do. Like building muscle - begin with a light weight you can handle. Increase the repetitions and increase the frequency until your muscles grow and you can handle more weight. Then repeat the process with greater weight. Frequency will make up for a lack of power initially. By working with a light weight - taking small steps - you will increase your faith.

Your goal is to increase your faith; to nurture belief in yourself, confidence you can succeed. Little by little, baby step by baby step, you will strengthen your faith. The stronger your faith - the more you leave to life and to divine intelligence - the greater the possibilities.

To begin establishing a means, a method, a habit of moving (taking action) in the right direction, progress through these steps:

1. YOU ARE NOT ALONE; DO NOT ATTEMPT TO GO IT ALONE.

Where two or more gather, spiritual power multiplies.

Build a mastermind group.

Form a team. Surround yourself with positive, active, growing people; people you respect, admire and aspire to be like. In building your mastermind group you should look for the absolute best people you can get to join you on a mutually supportive journey.

Your first task is to determine who to journey with (First Who, Then What).

The likely candidates for your initial mastermind group are not expected to be family members or even close friends. Not that you should distance or disassociate yourself from family or friends - just remember, you are looking for a new source of inspiration and a new source of motivation to help you move in a new direction. This means making some new friends, people with different experiences, different perspectives, and different skills and abilities.

Find at least one, but preferably two or three positive, supportive people who are motivated to work with you for your mutual benefit.

Individually and as a group commit to supporting each other over a specified period of time - at least initially, say twelve weeks or so. If all goes well this could be the core of your long-term mastermind group.

Your ultimate intent is to change course, and to grow and usher in more abundant, exciting, and invigorating circumstances. While this is your initial motivation your underlying purpose must be to establish and maintain a team - a mastermind group where all participants benefit. Your mastermind group should allow each participant to gain from the association. This means your purpose must be to help other people grow and become- fulfill their potential. To the degree you are successful helping other people excel, you will transform.

So before you start recruiting, determine what it is you bring to the table. Do you have unique skills and abilities to offer? You, for sure have a unique perspective, but is it a positive one?

If you don't have unique talents to offer then you are going to have to commit to adding value some other way. Are you going to be the positive social force to hold the team together? Are you going to provide the discipline to focus the mastermind group during routine meetings? Will you coordinate schedules, set agendas, and solicit commitments? Though you may not be the creative idea person, you can provide the muscle and the glue that keeps the group together and generating value.

Write out a mission statement for the mastermind group. Specify what general task you intend for this group to accomplish and suggest a tangible purpose - why the task is relevant, important, and achievable. Define expected commitments (meeting frequency, in person and via alternative media) over a determined length of time.

As an example:

> Your Initial Mission: To establish a mastermind group, consisting of at least four members, with the dedicated purpose of encouraging and assisting individual participants' personal and professional growth.

> Mastermind Group Mission: To serve as a mutually supportive group of positive individuals committed to growing personally and contributing to the development, maturing and professional advancement of all members of the group.

Mastermind Group Member Mission: To support and contribute to the growth and professional advancement of all members of the mastermind group.

Requirements:

Members Must Be:

Motivated to change and grow.

Positive, helpful, and encouraging.

Committed to the group.

Willing to take action to support and assist other group members.

Willing and able to meet regularly (in person and or via telephone or other communication medium) for one hour over the course of the next twelve weeks.

You may want to specify there are no financial commitments or obligations demanded or expected from this association.

You could tailor your mission statement to focus on personal growth or professional growth or both. It's your call initially. After establishing the group however, the focus should be a collective consensus. Likewise you'll want to ensure everyone is on board with the frequency and duration of the initial association. In other words - expect to revise you mission statement at the first meeting.

You must commit to meeting all the requirements you define for the specified period - no excuses. As you are initiating the mastermind group you have to lead and leadership requires commitment, discipline and follow-through.

Take the mission statement and participant requirements to someone you trust to provide appropriate feedback on how the statement reads. Does it convey the message you intend?

Once you are satisfied with the mission statement, move on to searching for some willing and valuable team members. Review your mission statement often (a couple of times a day) to ensure you stay on task and on target.

Now activate your network. You are looking for a few people who meet the requirements you defined, and who are accessible, available, and willing to be part of your group. You may not want to reveal to your closest family members and friends exactly what you are looking for. You may get some volunteers who feel obligated to you and to whom you will feel obligated. These people may not fulfill the commitments you have prescribed.

The ultimate goal is movement in a new, positive direction, so seek some new, positive allies. Ask for referrals from friends and family and from acquaintances you respect and trust. Energize your social networking contacts (assuming you have a virtual network: Facebook, Linked-In, etc.). Post messages on Craigslist or engage in some conversations through specialized groups.

If you are seeking maximum diversity (that is perspectives, professions, and approaches to life) do some research on which spiritual backgrounds, skill sets, life experiences, education levels, and degree of professional success would be most advantageous to assemble in your group. Again, energize your network to locate potential candidates. Find out what associations have chapters in your area. Seek those organizations out. You are looking for referrals to lead you to people who you will enjoy talking to, learning from, and helping for a period of time.

You can expect, if your temporary mastermind group meets with some success, these new acquaintances will become your friends and possibly remain in your life for a very long time. So choose carefully and choose well.

Let your intuition guide you to the talent, the expertise, and the motivation your mastermind group requires. Be aware right from the start if you harbor fear, or are timid about this task. Your first mission is to grow beyond the fear.

You are not necessarily seeking a band of high achievers and aggressive personalities. Assuredly those people can assist you on your journey, but what you need at the start is a means to begin building confidence and nurturing faith. If you don't have a track record of soaring accomplishments and an endless wellspring of positive motivation, then attempt to secure small wins. With every step forward, with every little obstacle breached you will begin to reveal your true potential. You will begin to nurture faith - in yourself, in other people, and in life.

Faith is the ultimate power. With faith you can achieve anything.

You are where you are now because of the choices you have made in the past. Make new choices. These choices will open up new perspectives. You will see new opportunities. Keep on going. Little by little your fear will succumb to a growing faith, a faith in unlimited possibility - the truth that will set you free.

For you who continue to read but resist this idea - the notion of forming a dynamic mastermind group with real live members (which is the best action to take), here is an alternative:

If all you can find is one other individual, or if finding one ally in your venture is not possible, you can still form your own council.

Over the course of the next few days select from six to twelve individuals, living or deceased, whom you admire and respect (typically notable historical figures, but it could be relatives). Ideally these are people with the traits and experiences you would like to grow into.

Collect biographical sketches and pictures of these achievers and guides. Assemble the pictures on one piece of paper or board. If you wish, you can hang 8" x 11" framed pictures of each person on a wall in what will be your routine meeting space. These people together are your board of directors.

This is your council of confidantes. Draw on the wisdom, the kindness, the ingenuity and the resolve of the members of your spiritual mastermind group. Consult and commune with these individuals as you would with live people in your presence. Imagine vividly, in as much detail and in accordance with the traits and peculiarities of each member, how each person would act.

By exercising your imagination and concentrating your effort these men and women will come alive for you. Meet together and adhere to the same commitments you set out in your mastermind mission statement. Set an agenda for your meetings, find a quiet space, and partition some uninterrupted time to focus your mind. Conduct a spirited, supportive, mutually beneficial board meeting.

At your first meeting, with the advice and counsel of your mastermind group members, validate the specific mission for the team. Reach consensus on the mission statement. In your imagination, and to the most minute detail possible, have every member sign your declaration of intent.

You will be meeting with these noble souls routinely over the next number of weeks. Come to know them, their likes, their dislikes, and their perspectives regarding any number of things. Their collective wisdom and insight will help guide you on your journey.

From now on I won't make any distinction between a mastermind group consisting of flesh and blood participants and one assembled from the spiritual dimension. You are not alone. Your mastermind group is one defined set of people working on your behalf. They are not the only ones.

Your weekly mastermind group meetings can be over a meal, at someone's house, or by way of a communications medium. Each person on the team will determine a path, a goal, or an objective, and will move toward it. It is the purpose of the mastermind group not to set the goals for, or judge, individual members. It is the mastermind's purpose to help participants think creatively, settle on actions steps, and hold themselves accountable to execute what each person determines to be their course. The group is to support each other and assist each other in advancing in a worthwhile direction.

2. PRAY OR MEDITATE. IF YOU DON'T LIKE THOSE WORDS: THINK.

You are embarking on a magnificent voyage. You are setting sail and changing direction. Moving from fear to faith.

Small steps consistently taken in the right direction will take you to your destination. Starting your journey is an awesome, life-changing event.

Absolute faith requires absolute control of your thoughts. When you have absolute control of your thoughts you will recognize that everything you experience is of your own doing. You will control your focus, your feelings, and shape the results you experience in your daily life. You will be totally responsible and totally in control.

The distance from where you are now to this perfect truth is not as far as you may think. You must be willing to intentionally move in that direction. As difficult as this may be, for now, let go of what you think you are. Do not burden yourself with preconceived notions of religion or God, rules or restrictions. Your conception of ultimate reality, whatever it is, limits God. Your perception of God limits you. If your conception of God - divine will, infinite intelligence - is one of fire and brimstone, judging and vengeful, you are holding yourself back.

This small step now is to move beyond fear. Release any tendency to judge.

Your task is to nurture faith. Start by setting aside time on a daily basis to be alone with your thoughts.

While thinking comes naturally (that is, a typical person entertains tens of thousands of thought impulses each day), thinking "deliberately" is the hardest work human beings undertake.

For your initial session, quietly and privately ponder your shift in direction. Ask the power beyond the confines of your flesh and blood - the source - to assist you as you journey. The truth is - the source - has, is, and always will be assisting you. You, however, are free to ignore any or all assistance offered.

Here today, right now - ask for help.

Ask these questions and think:

> Who am I?
> Why am I here?
> Where shall I go?
> Which way from here?

Ultimately you will ask for what you want to become, to possess and to experience, but for now seek a smaller objective. Ask the power outside of your physical body, the power outside physical reality, to help you remain open to change, and help you become impervious to fear.

Ask the power greater than your finite nature and limited intellect to reveal your true potential and open your mind and heart to unlimited opportunity. Nothing gets better until you change - ask the power to help you allow yourself to change; to welcome new experiences, new opportunities, new circumstances.

Your life is a journey. You're going somewhere. You might as well go somewhere grand.

Remember, you have not been abandoned. Your true nature is much more than you can understand in your current state. Everything that happens, happens for a reason and it's all good. The sooner you let go of what you have now - your current attitudes, experiences and circumstances - the sooner you will find and experience new and better things.

To travel requires action. You must move. To go where you want to go, you must control your advance (not just react to events). Ask the power to help you persist in always taking the next step - on blind faith if nothing else. Your next step leads you one step closer to a worthwhile destination.

Over the course of the next week, set aside fifteen minutes each day to pray, meditate, or ponder these questions. As you persist, answers will start to become clear.

3. COUNT YOUR BLESSINGS AND BUILD AN ATTITUDE OF GRATITUDE.

Make a list of all your attributes and experiences and all the people and things in your life you are grateful for. Include what or who you are grateful for and why. Building a comprehensive list will take some time over a few days. Work on the list, then put it aside. In a day or two new items will come to mind to add to and refine your list.

At your next mastermind meeting, discuss your list with the team. Use the session to brainstorm and add more points as you uncover them.

Refer to this list often. Post the list somewhere prominent in your home and place of work. You want to see this list daily. You have a lot to be thankful for - don't forget these things.

Your task now is to begin changing your mindset from one of lack to one abundance; from one of discontent to one of appreciation; from one of dissatisfaction to one of gratitude. You must be glad about what you have and be glad about what is to come.

The nuance to keep in mind here is that desire for change motivates you to progress. Just remember that what you have and experience in your life now is the product of your past choices. It's all good.

Be thankful you are a success. You have succeeded getting where you are today.

Find joy in the journey. Stop judging and give thanks.

Create a poster, a mural, or a drawing that will serve as a daily reminder of all you are thankful for.

Continue to study your blessings all week.

Remember, you are building your faith. Ultimately your faith will allow you to realize your greatest intention - your purpose for being. For now, however, you are just beginning your exercise routine. Substitute frequency (increased intervals for short periods) for heavy weights. By persisting your mind will come under your control and circumstances will begin to change.

4. CONFRONT THE BRUTAL FACTS.

Where you are now is not nearly as important as where you are heading. However, if you are struggling to determine clearly where it is you want to go, start by deciding what you don't want.

The point here is to look around. Honestly assess who you are and where you are.

Break out a writing pad. In bullet form, produce a complete and accurate description of the person you are and the circumstances you are now experiencing. Hold nothing back. Do not judge any aspect of your current condition. You are collecting and representing the facts of your current situation.

List your vital statistics and more:

Personal:

Age.

Height and Weight.

Fitness Level (if you have specific measures (run/swim time) include those.)

Education (degrees and academic certifications).

Skills (nonprofessional skills: hobbies; talents; etc.).

Attitude (honestly assess whether you exhibit a generally positive and open attitude toward life or if you tend to display a negative and restrictive attitude. Are you a "glass half empty" or "glass half full" type of person?).

Hours per week devoted to personal maintenance and growth (health and fitness, self-development, hobbies, education).

Professional:

> Current career field.
>
> Current position (job title).
>
> Hours per week (include commuting).
>
> Salary, Benefits, Perks.
>
> Vocational and professional certifications.
>
> Vocational and professional skills.

Social *(the more removed, the less intimate the people are, list numbers and categories; don't worry about names and specific roles)*:

> Married / Single / Divorced / Parent.
>
> Family (immediate and extended).
>
> Hours per week (family time).
>
> Friends (close and not so close).
>
> Boss(es), Co-workers, Employees.
>
> Associates.
>
> Customers, Clients, Patients.
>
> Hours per week devoted to each category.

Financial:

> Home Owner or Renter.
>
> Physical Assets (house, car, other possessions. Don't list every item, just the ones you would consider valuable).
>
> Savings (cash in various accounts).
>
> Investments (list amounts by category).
>
> Hours per week devoted to money management.

Spiritual:

Religious Denomination / Status (active participant or taking a break).

State of conviction (sure / unsure: of what?).

Predominant State (calm / peace or fear / anxiety? More tears than laughter? More conflict or collaboration?).

Hours per week devoted to spiritual development.

Physical Surroundings:

Location.

Places you routinely visit (parents, vacation sites, etc.).

Circumstances:

Describe in a summary paragraph your current situation.

Are you on cruise control; in a rut; getting by; feeling overwhelmed; stalled?

What consumes most of your time; energy; and attention?

As mentioned, it doesn't matter where you are now - it only matters where you are going. But, by going through this exercise you can begin to see more clearly what your past choices have produced and where your past choices have led.

You have created the reality you are now living, by your own choices. Don't fret, don't worry, don't despair. It is in fact time to celebrate. Remember the things you listed to be thankful for - pull out that list. Your current reality is only a temporary condition - a condition you can change immediately. Focusing on the details of your current situation, you may even expand your "things to be grateful about" list. However, by cataloging the circumstances of your life - the result of choices you made in the past - you can isolate and identify some things and circumstances you do not want.

Start to become absolutely clear on your new direction. You are now going to make new choices and create an entirely new, abundant, joyful reality.

5. DEFINE YOUR GOAL / OBJECTIVE / AIM (WHAT DO YOU WANT?).

This step - determining your direction - is the single most important act of your life.

What do you want to have, be, do?

You have, in fact, engaged in this activity a multitude of times in the past. Most often, however, your goal selection mechanism has been on autopilot. You have been engaging the world like an object. You respond to stimuli as need arises. Your choice now is to alter your state from object to actor. You are going to deliberately and intentionally take control of your life by selecting a worthy destination - an objective that measures up to your potential.

Keep in mind, we operate in a world of "nouns" - stuff, but in reality, what matters most, what makes life are "verbs" - actions and experiences. For everything you want to have, be, or do - your ultimate purpose will be to achieve some feeling. Every task you intend to accomplish, every goal you in fact achieve produces a feeling. Feelings are magnetic. Through small measures generate good feeling then build some momentum and grow.

Before you get enamored with selecting targets and tasks, take some time to commune alone with your thoughts. Pray, meditate, think. Ask that power outside of your mortal being to guide you in making right choices. Ask that you may choose wisely the most appropriate and fulfilling purposes. These purposes will dictate your direction and destination.

Your guides will assuredly help.

Fixing in your mind and in your heart, a worthwhile purpose will determine how you focus your thoughts. A worthwhile purpose, one that aligns with your life purpose will invigorate you. You are on a mission. To go from here to some worthwhile, fulfilling there. Every task you undertake, every task you accomplish has a purpose. The purpose is why you live.

Do you remember the last time you felt enthusiastic, highly motivated, joyful? The right goal will help bring these emotions back to you. You must be moving in a direction that draws you, that stimulates you, that inspires you. Anything less is sure not to invoke your full potential.

You want to be on the track of growth and excitement and joy. Seek the right train.

Ultimate faith can be likened to an obsession. To illustrate this point I'll draw on a negative example most people are familiar with: an addict. An addict is obsessed with the object of their addition: alcohol, drugs, sex, gambling, weight. We think of addicts as people who are addicted to self-destructive behavior. But addicts who are addicted to life, growth, and love are super high achievers. This is the type of addict you want to be.

You don't want to be an addict obsessed with self-destruction. You want to cultivate an obsession with life, with growth, with advancement. "Passion" is the word for inspired state. People who are passionate take inspired action.

Moving from fear to faith will take you from helpless to powerful. Getting there requires motivation. You must become obsessed with your goal. You become obsessed by building new habits - habits of focusing thought. The more you concentrate your mind on your worthwhile objective the more motivation will emerge.

You are attempting to create an upward spiral. Feed your obsession, in small doses at first. Eventually, as you persist, you will generate small currents of electricity and in time irresistible power to achieve everything you desire.

Back to work.

Begin drafting your Life Mission Statement. A Life Mission Statement is one of purpose and destiny. This statement is likely to encompass many areas and ultimately will be measured by contribution and growth. A Life Mission Statement is going to take some effort to compile and will evolve over time.

To get going, and make some small advances, begin with tangible, definable, questions. Determine where you want your life to go:

What about your current reality do you want to change?

What are you best at? What comes easily to you?

What do you really enjoy doing? Where does your passion lie?

Where do you want to be five, ten, or twenty years from now?

Do you want to:
  Be fit and healthy?

  Have a big, happy family?

  Be positive, giving, nurturing?

Be financially independent?

Be rich?

Travel to exotic locales?

Run your own company?

Attain a position of trust and importance?

Write or type out your answers. List what you want to have, be, or do.

You are drawing a contrast between your current life and the life you intend.

Sort the wheat from the chaff. Identify those things in your current circumstances you want to eliminate or grow away from, and identify the circumstances you want to grow toward. Describe your perfect reality five, ten, or twenty years from now in exact detail.

Create a "dream board." Select pictures of what you want from magazines or brochures, or print them off the internet (people, places and things in your future ideal reality; achievements, accomplishments, changes in attributes such as fitness, health, and attitude).

Your dream board pictures represent your future reality.

As you lay out your goals, make sure you consider what you would do if you were guaranteed to succeed. It is time to dream big.

After you have carefully thought through your intermediate goals (as opposed to your Life Mission Statement), write each goal out in a precise way:

- In Present Tense (as if you accomplished it already)

- State Positively (not "I will lose weight," but "I weigh...")

- Specific and Measurable (so you can recognize achievement)

- Reasonable and Challenging (out of your comfort zone but not beyond your faith)

- Include a Deadline (for urgency and motivation)

Now step back and consider this list of wants. Think again "why" you want each of these things. The goal you have defined is your task to accomplish - "why" you are going to achieve that task is your purpose.

Internalize your goals by reviewing and speaking aloud each task at least twice daily. Rewrite your top three goals every day. Remember, frequency substitutes for, and develops, power.

Enthusiastically (as if you have the object of your desire now) discuss your highest priority goals with confidants (likely members of your mastermind group). This list of goals represents the new reality you are creating.

6. MOTIVATION.

Desire is the seed of motivation. In our affluent, opulent world, however, it's too easy to settle for getting by. We rationalize satisfaction with the status quo. Comfort and convenience become the standard, the norm. We give up on realizing our true potential.

Motivation, or desire, is the factor that determines your willingness to select a direction - to chart a course. Motivation is also the impetus for the speed of advance. No motivation: other forces are in charge - you respond and react - comfort and security are the goal. You constantly mull around. Your life is a chore. Weak motivation: you will choose a direction, but constantly be overwhelmed by circumstances. Running free, your thoughts create circumstances similar to those you face now. Your advance is slow - your attention and energy are scattered. Strong motivation: you choose a direction and focus your thoughts. Energy increases as you move toward your aim. You create your own reinforcing spiral of success. You advance quickly and deliberately.

It's time for you to assess what you have to work with.

> What kind of track record do you have?

> What have you accomplished / achieved at any point in your life?

> Where have you succeeded?

> What have you had the desire and motivation, the discipline and commitment to complete at some point in the past?

Create a list (look back at your current situation bullet list).

Using your newly composed list as your standard, and knowing yourself as well as you do: Are you self-motivated?

You have definitely accomplished things. You have succeeding getting where you are. The question is, can you believe, and therefore achieve, more substantial things?

If you have evidence of some accomplishment in the past you can build on that example for motivation. Do you remember what it took to achieve what you did?

You need to reclaim some of that discipline to start out on a new course. The best course to set out on is to do something you are good at and love doing. If you have determined you are not self-motivated - how are you going to fuel your motivation, stoke your desire? Remember, everything you do in life has a purpose (has a "why"). If you are not self-motivated you have weak "whys."

Create a list of "WHYs" to compliment your dream board. "Why" is key. Organize your goals by category of purpose - your "whys." You won't make any progress unless your reasons (your "whys") are strong enough to propel you forward. Review your "WHYs" along with your objectives multiple times daily.

If you stop advancing, it's because your "WHY" is weak. Strengthen it. Consult the lists you made of what your current circumstances are. Review what you have to be thankful for. Then focus on your dream board. Your faith is still too weak to overcome your internal resistance. Commit to taking a small, easy step and keep moving.

Use you mastermind group to help keep yourself focused and motivated. You are engaged in mental activity here. With more exercise your faith is going to get stronger. You are working to gain control of your thoughts. Everyday take more control of your life. Focus your thoughts on your chief aim.

Consider if you need a coach. You could expand your field of advocates by hiring a coach - to help you achieve a specific goal, overcome a specific obstacle, or assist you as a life coach.

Up to this point you have been drawing upon power greater than your own. You have assembled a group dedicated to realizing progress. You are routinely thinking (praying and meditating). You have selected a course and assessed your willingness to advance. Now it's time to set expectations.

You are still alive and you aren't going anywhere anytime soon, so you might as well advance along your new course. Persist moving in a new direction. It's all, success or failure, in your mind.

7. ANTICIPATE OBSTACLES - ELIMINATE EXCUSES.

So far, you have established a mastermind group consisting of dedicated members you can assist and who can assist you on your journey; you have consulted the deepest recesses of your mind and the power of ultimate reality through prayer, meditation and focused thinking; you have counted your blessings, realizing how much you have to be thankful for; you have pulled back the veil of your current situation, honestly assessing the brutal facts; you have carefully selected a new destination and a new direction in which to travel; and you have checked the fuel in your tank. Now it is time to begin planning.

Any road, anywhere, is bound to be littered with obstacles big and small. The most obvious impediment from where you are now to wherever it is you intend to go is the distance between the two points.

Let's take an automobile trip as an example. After you have selected a destination, you know the transit from start to finish is not instantaneous. The trip will take some time. Your vehicle must be up to the task, you need an appropriate amount of fuel and you need a plan (either you know the way or you must have an accurate map or directions you can follow).

You could assume the lighting and weather conditions will be optimum, the sun shining (but not in your eyes), the pavement dry, traffic will not be a factor, no construction along the way, etc. But for any except the shortest road trip, this would be poor planning.

Instead you are best served preparing for as many contingencies as possible. You would calculate the time to travel the distance under optimal conditions, and then factor in likely delays. Being well prepared you would carry the necessary supplies to manage a flat tire or a vehicle malfunction. You would anticipate congested roads, construction and other possible delays as well. Prudent planning will ensure you get to your destination.

A road trip requires a degree of planning and preparation. Why should the journey of your life be any different? You know where you are and you know where you are headed. This task is to consider and list every conceivable obstacle you might encounter along the way to your goal.

The obstacles comprising your list might range from external obstructions such as a lack of physical resources or information and knowledge, to a shortage of strategic allies, to internal impediments such as maintaining focus, discipline, and motivation, and overcoming your own resistance and fear.

Compile a matching list of every conceivable excuse that you can imagine as to why you might not be able to achieve your goal. Spend some time reviewing each entry on both your lists. You might even take your list to your mastermind group and discuss the inventory with your trusted confidants. Weigh each obstacle and corresponding excuse against the purpose you identified for achieving your goal. Consider "why" you intend to move to your destination against every alibi you have imagined. If your "why" does not overcome every obstacle - your focus must turn to your motive.

Obstacles spring from one of two sources: 1) external obstacles are a means to challenge you and help you grow, be and become; 2) internal obstacles are your resistance to progress, resistance to change, resistance to growth.

Which category does each of the obstacles and excuses fall into? If the obstacle is external - full speed ahead. Every step you take toward your goal summons forces in the universe to help you succeed. As long as you are moving in the right direction, heaven and earth will cooperate and aid your journey. With courage, patience and persistence you will come upon a means to overcome every external obstacle you encounter. Take the next step.

If the obstacle and excuse is internal, realize the obstacle does not really exist. That the impediment is even an obstacle at all is because you are making it one. You have absolute control over your internal reality. You, in fact, project your internal reality out into the world. If you are haunted by obstacles originating from within, as mentioned before, do what you can do with greater frequency. Frequency will substitute for power.

Confront the Four Horsemen of your apocalypse. The Four Horsemen are labels for the internal impediments people routinely allow to dominate their lives. These Four Horsemen are the main excuses for living a mediocre existence. The Four Horsemen are Complacency, Confusion, Arrogance, and Fear.

Complacency is the satisfaction with the status quo. What one has now is "good enough." The mental gymnastics of complacency are usually calculations of effort versus reward. Is the expected outcome or result of a given action worth the cost? Lack of motivation or ambition is one state only the individual can overcome. You can lead a horse to water, but you can't make it drink.

Confusion is a factor for nearly everyone not heading in the right direction. The issue here is in knowing which way to go. Lost in the maze of this physical reality, it is easy to become disoriented and confused. Sometimes the signs and the circumstances combine to produce a direction that seems feasible, workable, and laudable, but in fact leads the individual astray. The way to address confusion is by following the steps outlined here in this chapter. By seeking one finds. Seek the right path.

Arrogance is either the manifestation of ignorance or fear. The arrogant person assumes a theoretical position of power, which he or she exhibits as self-righteousness. This person is lost in the weeds, but is absolutely convinced that their limited perspective is all-knowing (at least as far as current circumstances are concerned) and true. The other type of arrogance is really an elaborate ruse to hide fear. In an effort to appear confident and strong the arrogant belittles whomever he or she can. This is a dismal attempt to build themselves up by knocking other people down. Never a good strategy.

Fear is a wholly psychological projection into the future. Fear is the anticipation of pain or loss, real or imagined. Fear is a current condition, a mental state the individual creates predicting the future. Fear, in a sense, is a trick of time travel. A person looks into the future and imagines that what is to come is troubling. This imagining induces a visceral response of resistance - fear. Fear is the expectation that change will be negative. While pain and loss are elements of this physical reality, fear need not be. Approaching change with the expectation of advance, improvement, growth, will go a long way toward eliminating the source of fear.

To overcome fear that has already set in, however, takes a willingness to observe and embrace your feelings and your thoughts. Fear is a mental state that generates powerful feelings. If you find yourself succumbing to fear, adjust your condition. Do not resist the feelings of fear - embrace them, explore them, expose them. Recognize and accept that you are feeling fear. Realize every tingle, every shiver, every bit of tightening that washes through your body. Explore how fear feels.

As you embrace the emotion of fear - not to defeat it, but to understand in an experiential way what the state feels like in the moment - consider what condition, in the future, fear is reacting to. Are you anticipating loss or pain?

The state of fear is a connection of your mental time travel and a judgment you levy on an expected outcome. Realizing this is an intellectual exercise and recognizing the components of the fear you harbor will help to alleviate it. Fear will not subside, however, until one or both of these conditions are met:

> 1) You modify your expectation about the future - the change (even if painful) will ultimately not be bad.

Or

> 2) You act, despite the fear, and move. As you come upon the instant you dread, action will reduce the impact of fear. Action can and will overcome the limitations of the intellect (the factory generating fear).

The key, the essential ingredient, is motive. Do you desire to grow, to be, to become despite the trials of internal storms? Take the next step, despite how you feel and you just might find, what you feared is actually a source of growth, a means of becoming, a catalyst for success.

These Four Horsemen of your apocalypse summarize the barriers to moving forward. These four characteristics can be reduced to one psychological impediment: fear.

Life is a journey. Get moving in the right direction and you'll find life is a journey to fulfillment - to joy. Anticipate obstacles. Wrestle with the obstacles in your mind before you set out - because even out there, on the dusty road, the obstacles are, will and only can be, in your mind. Keep moving in the right direction and ask yourself: What would I do if I weren't afraid?

8. ASSUME RESPONSIBILITY / CLAIM YOUR POWER.

No one can do it for you. People can encourage you, celebrate every little victory with you, even offer you all kinds of advantages in life, but no one can live your life for you. No one can make you grow. Only you can fulfill your potential. Only you experience and feel your life.

You get to be born into this world and you get to die. These two seminal events are the alpha and the omega of your contemporary journey. You chose to come here and you will chose to transition again. Why not take control of the journey in between?

As we have described, discussed and considered multiple times - life is change. And change is an inside job. The question bears repeating here: Are you up to the task?

You likely listed, in your catalog of excuses, all those forces, circumstances, people and institutions you, at times, believe have control of your life. The economy, politics, geography, your physical appearance and stature, your intellect, your skills and physical prowess - you contend these conditions limit you. Well, the truth is you possess absolute power. What you need to do is stop giving it away.

You are familiar with laws of nature - things like gravity, and cycles, and energy transference. Learn these most important laws of nature:

> Life intends to grow (you are meant to contribute to the purpose of life).

> You possess the power to fashion your own experiences and circumstances; thoughts become things.

> This is a collective journey (you are not alone).

Contribution generates reward; give to receive.

Power cannot be had without responsibility.

Power and responsibility are two sides of the same coin. You can have absolute power, if you want it. To assume absolute power you must assume absolute responsibility.

Instead of claiming our power, we seek to absolve ourselves of responsibility and by so doing, give away our power. We lament our weakness, but by ducking responsibility we get to relish in the empty thrill of placing blame.

To wield the power that is your birthright, that is your asset, that is your destiny, accept complete and total responsibility for who you are, what you are and where you are. You are responsible for everything in your life. Do not concern yourself about every little detail of life. Just know that how you interpret what you experience, and what you judge as good and bad, are under your control.

Write out, in big, bold letters, the statement, "I AM RESPONSIBLE." and plaster it around your living and work spaces. Accept responsibility for your life and reclaim your power.

9. FAITH - BELIEF.

Every thought you have considered, and every action you have taken up to this point has been intended to build your faith.

Thoughts are things; powerful things. Thoughts are the forces through which people manipulate and manufacture experiences - generate feelings. As you conceive and nurture thought you fuel the creation of that thought in physical reality. What you seek, seeks you.

You become what you think about.

Reshape your world by disciplining your thought. Cultivate an attitude of gratitude. No matter what is happening around you (the results of past thoughts), remember you control what happens within you. And you control what the future brings. All circumstances, all events, all obstacles are opportunities for you to grow.

We often use the words "faith" and "belief" interchangeably, but then we ascribe faith to another, distant realm; one divorced from everyday existence. Faith is abiding knowledge in things not seen. Just because it's not seen doesn't mean it's not real. You will see what you seek if you persist, if you persevere, if you continue your journey. Belief is literally what you live by; what you do that demonstrates your faith. If you intend to create a new reality - do new things, take new action. By persisting with small positive actions your faith will grow.

Frequency substitutes for power. Take small, reasonable steps frequently. If you currently believe you control nothing but your thoughts, persist in attempting to control your thoughts. You see, controlling your thoughts will translate into controlling everything you encounter.

Devote some quality time daily (at least fifteen minutes) to visualizing the object of your desire. Remember that goal you painstakingly determined, see it, feel it as real, here and now. Design your own "self-talk" script. Commit that script to memory by writing it out five times a day. The script should be your goal. Your goal is the circumstance you intend that will result in the feelings you desire. Include the attributes you exhibit and possess as you continue to grow.

For instance:

"I am happily married, with four children, living in a magnificent house we own free and clear. We are financially free, stewards of abundant resources, effective leaders in our community. I am intelligent, resourceful, strong and compassionate. My efforts bring forth a great harvest as I continually strive to fulfill my full potential."

Influence your subconscious through autosuggestion.

10. CULTIVATE A HABIT OF ACTION.

Ours is a dualistic reality. Every state has an opposite, and every force has a countervailing force. I like to think of it as we live in binary world. Since life is the experience of constant change, you have two, and only two, choices in life: 1) act, or 2) resist.

Predispose yourself to act.

Move toward your dream, your goal, your aim. Success requires commitment. Success in life is an "all in" venture. You cannot expect to realize your potential or even achieve a small goal without action.

Action is faith empowered. Action empowers thought. You may recall the debate in the early Christian church about faith versus acts. One side claimed salvation was a matter of faith, their opponents challenged salvation was a matter of good works. The truth is, actions are the manifestation of faith in this physical reality. People's faith is expressed through action. Without action there is no faith. Just like you can't get to the second floor without overcoming gravity (walking up the stairs, jumping, scaling a ladder, climbing a rope), faith is only real when it manifests through action. The details of how faith manifests, is not the concern. To get to the second floor overcome gravity - just act. To possess faith you must act.

If you don't feel you have the faith necessary to complete the action steps needed to achieve your goal - do not despair. You will build faith, and overcome the inhibition of intellect, by acting, despite or as if. Act, even in little measures. By persisting you will build faith. If you are struggling controlling your mind - get your body working for you. Take consistent, persistent action in the direction of your goals. Every act you complete strengthens your faith.

Make a list of small, simple tasks you can complete daily. Things like: studying your dream board; reviewing your list of "why's"; physical exercises after getting out or before getting in bed; sending an email greeting to a friend; giving thanks and counting your blessings. Add these physical acts to your daily routine. Action will trump resistance. Commit to completing these tasks for twenty-one days in a row. It takes approximately twenty-one days to internalize and condition a new habit. Find some means of recording your daily completion of these physical acts over the next twenty-one days. If you discover you skipped a day, start again. Persist and prevail. Form a new habit and strengthen your faith.

If time constraints are an issue (your day is already chocked full of activities), replace less productive tasks with more productive tasks. Building your faith, focusing on your worthwhile objective, is the most productive thing you can do. Promise yourself that you will not go to sleep until the tasks you have committed to are complete. Cultivate a habit of action. You are a person of action.

11. DEFINE BABY STEPS.

You don't need a map from where you are to your final destination. All you really need is a direction and a willingness to advance. However, let's review the baby steps:

1) Commit to helping someone else grow (mastermind group).

2) Pray by asking for new experiences and new circumstances.

3) Count your blessings (cultivate an attitude of gratitude).

4) Confront your reality.

5) Focus at least twice daily on your goal, objective, aim (feel yourself already having achieved your desire).

6) Reinforce your passion (focus on why you want the change - get excited - feel the passion).

7) Obstacles, like excuses, are made in your head.

8) Accept full responsibility for who you are and how you feel.

9) Focus your thoughts on your new reality.

10) Take action every day - become a doer.

These baby steps are turning you in a new direction. Focus on your goal.

To reach your goal, what is the next thing you must do - not a grand thing - not a long-term thing - what is the next small thing you can do now to advance yourself toward your goal?

A master plan at this point may be helpful, or may be intimidating. You've already wrestled with the potential obstacles. As you move forward, as you advance, what you need to succeed is moving toward you. Be open to the journey. Embrace each requirement as you encounter it. Every moment is an opportunity for growth. Focus on the task at hand until you complete it. Then lock your gaze again firmly on your objective. If you can't find the way - feel your way.

Your road map, your blueprint, for success is ultimately a series of baby steps. If you completed the activities already prescribed in this chapter you have taken a number of baby steps. Having your goal firmly in your mind, sketch out the few steps that will lead you closer to your goal. List these baby steps out as far as you can see.

While this list connotes a map of sorts, don't worry about the multitudes of instances between now and your future, fulfilled reality. Start today embracing what you have before you - baby steps. With the innocence of a child you enter the kingdom. It's as simple as that.

12. TAKE THE NEXT STEP.

If you are still breathing you have some life left to live. Decide to make that life worthwhile. Your journey is filled with opportunity. Look for and seize the opportunity. Persevere by taking the next step in faith. You need not take any giant leap. Do what you are ready for. All you need to do is take that next baby step and give thanks.

Be thankful for what you are, for what you have, for what you are releasing, and for what you are receiving. Ask for what you want (pray, meditate, focus), and then receive (act). Release the old, move in the direction of the new, and the universe will meet you more than halfway.

Use these tactics and techniques to help move from fear to faith.

Life intends for you to advance. Life is designed to promote your wellbeing. Work with life, not against it.

Cutting to the chase, requires action. Select a direction and move. If good feelings grow you are heading in the right direction.

Keep moving - keep advancing - keep laughing - keep loving. Life is not more than that - for that is glorious and magnificent.

Success 101: How Life Works

7
MONEY, POLITICS AND ECONOMICS

You may be thinking this is an odd subject - a chapter that seems out of place. After all, the objective of this volume is to stimulate personal growth. Yet to achieve your full potential as an individual, unless you live alone on a desert island, you live among other people and are connected to society and its institutions. So, you must deal with complex social systems.

The vast majority of human beings live in a social setting. We depend on other people, and other people depend on us.

Personal relationships make life, and relationships define society.

What are the three primary drivers of society? Money, politics and economics.

After relationships, economics and politics are the two social dimensions of life with the most influence and impact. Politics and economics set the conditions for how much money people have. Politics is fundamentally about the allocation and management of power in a civilization. Economics is the domain of production, distribution and consumption in the physical world.

The forces and factors of both politics and economics drive and control people the world over, from cradle to grave. Politics establishes the social rules we live and play by, while economics defines the processes through which people manipulate and allocate resources within the environment and attend to issues of supply and demand.

Since the focus of most people, most of the time, is on the physical component of this reality (as opposed to the spiritual or ethereal dimensions), most people believe in, respond to, and devote considerable mental, emotional and physical effort toward economic and political concerns. Surviving and thriving in a material world is paramount.

Politics is an element of all human interaction - from one-on-one encounters, to family dynamics, to community interactions, to the functioning of the state. Much of what we have covered in this book focuses on and addresses the sphere of the individual and the nature of power. Here we ratchet up the complexity - offering another perspective.

To further explore and explain how life works, this chapter highlights the relationship between the individual and the state, and the individual and the economy. Money facilitates the functioning of both politics and economics and serves as a means to keep score. Most people believe, erroneously, that politics and economics are purely functions of the material world. This is simply not true. Politics and economics are manifestations of our communal faith - how individuals collectively approach each other and attempt to address the conditions of this world.

POWER AND MATERIAL WEALTH

Ultimately the individual has access to absolute power. A human being is one with the source - divine intelligence, the font of all knowledge and all power. Rarely, however, does an individual avail him or herself of that access and use that power. Rather the individual, unwittingly or deliberately, confers his or her power to others (individuals or institutions), for what seem, at the time, to be reasonable advantages.

People forfeit power for two primary reasons:

1. To reduce demands on their time, energy and intellects (to make life easier).

2. To contribute to a collective system that advances their interests.

Normally people readily and willingly surrender power to reduce their load. They give power to another individual, organization or institution so that they don't have to be responsible for, or devote effort toward, certain actions or activities. These actions and activities range from household duties, to career demands, to the workings of the community, to maintaining order, securing the peace, and ensuring the welfare of society.

As we have considered before, power and freedom are perceived as universal values. Power and freedom are synonymous. Absolute power is absolute freedom. Absolute freedom is absolute power. Holding the consideration of the ultimate value - love - aside for the moment, there is nothing in this world people desire more than power and freedom. People covet both, crave both, and seek both, up and until they realize that power and freedom come with responsibility.

Absolute power and absolute freedom are accompanied by, are integrated with, and are amalgamations of the same singular authority. And unfortunately there are few things in life immature people (and most of us fall into this category) want less then responsibility. So as people run from responsibility, they inadvertently abandon power and freedom.

The second, but not nearly as dominant, reason for giving up personal power, is to advance self-interest by contributing to the collective good. Societies build and maintain systems to facilitate the functioning of social order. Each culture establishes and enforces certain measures to ensure citizens abide by and contribute to the social order. Some people throw in willingly, some begrudgingly, but all are compelled to comply with mandates imposed expressly for the common good. The functioning of any collective system requires each individual member devote some personal power to the common welfare.

Politics is the realm of these messy power dynamics.

Economics is the discipline concerned with the production, distribution and consumption of goods and services. Or, put another way, economics is concerned with the material welfare of humankind. Economics seeks to make sense of, arguably, the most pervasive and important earthly devotions of human intellect and effort – productive enterprise. For human beings are, at their essence, creators.

Economics attempts to explain the world of markets and labor, productivity and exchange, abundance and lack. The practices of production, manufacturing, trade and distribution - all functions of business (though not exclusively) - fall within the purview of economics.

Economics has been dubbed the "dismal science," as some believe economics fundamentally deals with the allocation of scarce or limited resources. This belief suggests there is never enough, and there are always,

always, always - haves and have-nots. No society has or can achieve a utopia for all its members - the physical world is, by nature, insufficient and lacking.

This "scarce resources" view, while predominant in economic circles, demonstrates an ignorance of the fundamental nature and functioning of this reality. Unfortunately we live with the blinders we affix about our eyes and the chains we gird ourselves with.

On the physical level of existence, people want and need goods and services to survive, to grow, and to prosper. The collective wisdom of individuals and society over time has established means to facilitate economic functions. People harvest plants, animals, and raw materials to feed, clothe, and shelter the multitudes, and supply every conceivable need. Through businesses, social ventures (non-profit), and government efforts people organize, combine resources and offer goods and services to meet the wants and needs of individuals and society at large. Goods and services range in composition from intellectual property, to the manual labor of men, women and children, to natural raw materials and plant stuffs, to manufactured goods.

Economics is the realm of stuff, labor and intellect - all very much influenced by politics.

For those people with their feet firmly planted on the ground, their focus on accumulating stuff, and their noses to the grindstone (most people), economics and politics are where it's at.

Exploring and appreciating economics and politics adds immeasurably to understanding how life works. Human beings are social creatures. We are not divisible. In the physical realm we are part of an environment and a social order that sustains us. Our political and economic systems are influenced by the divine whole, but are reflections of our collective wills. Our collective wills, however, are infected by the collective biases and collective weaknesses we share.

MONEY IS POWER? HAPPINESS?

Money, a medium of exchange, a unit of account, and a store of value, is one tool available to you for use in the material world. Money is governed by the processes of economics and politics. So the people who seek to satisfy material desires, seek to understand, engage in, or manipulate both economics and politics.

People believe money is the solution to all their problems. What about you? If only you had a million dollars, life would be bearable, interesting, enjoyable, maybe exhilarating. Some people assert with every waking breath that money, money, money is the answer to their prayers. Well is it?

As the concept of money evolved over the millennia – substituting agreements of value for things – money became a substitute for power. The words: "money," "power," "property" have evolved as a series of surrogates. With power the primordial desire and survival in a material world the paramount pursuit, money and power are always linked. Things, objects - property, possessions - became proxies for power. As more people trusted the functioning of money, over time money developed into a proxy for things.

The desire for power springs from a natural instinct to stabilize an unstable existence. Money has come to represent what we covet most - power. In a material world, where property is king, money is power!

After the need to survive the most pervasive force in the human psyche is the drive to gain power. We want to be in control, we want to be in charge – we want to be powerful. By securing prosperity for oneself and one's kin, people aren't necessarily looking for money - they are seeking the power and freedom money represents. They aren't searching for tangible things; they hunt for power. But to what end?

On the scale of universe's expanse, we are simple, relatively small and powerless creatures making our way in a material existence. We judge our surroundings and our success by what we can see, hear, touch, taste, and smell – this is, after all, a physical world. And in this physical world we see limited resources, limited time, and lots of competition. We have come to believe, by lifetimes of physical evidence, that our survival and success are dependent on our ability to compete for a share of the resource pie; to accumulate what we can, and thereby achieve some level of power over our existence.

Digging a little deeper leads to the question - Why do we want money?

In the final analysis it is not money, nor things, not even power that really matters; these are all means to an end. Life is ultimately all about experience - feelings - and the experiences we seek are about joy, growth, and fulfillment. We seek money and engage in economic activities and politics for power. But we seek power for happiness. Ultimately, it's all about happiness - good feelings.

Life is fleeting. We are on a temporary journey, and we are encouraged, guided, moved to act. What we seek is happiness. What we get is experience.

The challenge is making experience and happiness one and the same. Achieving this outcome is not a labor for money - it is a labor of love. Keep money, economics and politics in perspective. It doesn't matter how much stuff you possess, your goal in life is to fulfill your potential. Money and power are really only tools. What you seek, truly, is to build an abundant, fulfilled and fulfilling life. Don't waste time accumulating money when what you really desire is happiness.

Devote your time, energy and talents to the manufacture of joy, and money won't matter.

PEOPLE, NOT MONEY, MAKE THE WORLD GO ROUND

In industry, in finance, even in government, competitors apply the principles of supply and demand, production and consumption, leverage and compound interest. Nowhere in the physical world are immutable laws, predictability and certainty more sought after and valued than in business and markets.

Economists, academics, business consultants, and financial gurus alike seek to refine hypotheses and develop ever more exacting language and formulas in an attempt to demystify the workings of supposedly rational free markets. In their haste to uncover a path to fortune, the learned theorists overlook the most fundamental and significant aspect of money and markets - people.

If we were to attempt to assess the worth of all items with economic value in this world, from people to resources to ideas, we undoubtedly would arrive in the hundreds of trillions of dollars. The estimated value of everything, from real estate, to commodities, to personal, corporate or government owned property however, is not fixed. Values are in fact volatile expectations of worth. These expectations are held, not in a vault, not in a computer, not in a quarry, but in the minds of human beings.

The values of all things are determined by the wants and needs, by the desires, of human beings. A thing -

piece of property, a possession, a service - is only as valuable as what a person will pay for it. All values are set by needs, wants, or desires. These needs, wants, or desires constitute demand.

Conversely, human beings provide the motivation, the knowledge, and the labor to meet all types of economic demands - wants, needs, desires. The energy of ideas, thought alone, or combined by labor with natural resources, act to satisfy the seemingly insatiable desires of an ever-growing population. Desires are needs that are ultimately seeking fulfillment in feeling. The energy of desire creates or attracts circumstances to generate the intended feelings.

As no one is an island unto himself, people benefit from the time, energy and talent others apply to thought, production, distribution, and a myriad of other value added pursuits for sustenance and quality of life. People create, attract, and supply the products and services to satisfy wants and needs.

The component elements of markets or whole economies are: motivation and ideas, knowledge, labor, and physical resources. Economic pundits often focus erroneously on the tangible elements of the economic equation (physical resources and labor), while it is the intangible elements (motivation, ideas, and knowledge) that really matter. It is through these elements the physical world of effects interacts with the ethereal dimension of cause.

Physical resources are required to sustain living things. That accords with the laws and functioning of the physical environment - the rules of the game. Nothing happens however, for production, distribution, services or trade, without motivation. Motives are linked to thought, these in turn lead to labor - action. Someone, or most often a group, must do something to produce or provide a product or service to meet a specific need.

The dance of supply and demand is commonly recognized as a physical, material function. Actually however, it is both a vastly human undertaking and a mysteriously spiritual enterprise. The system we inhabit, drive and are driven by, is both beautiful in its simplicity and majestic in its complexity. It is much more than a mechanical system.

Beyond physical resources and labor, every human activity, every product or service developed or offered for trade is the result of the application of motivation, ideas, and knowledge. People are motivated to act. They employ labor and manipulate physical resources to fashion all means of viable products and services for personal use or trade. The more knowledge and innovation people dedicate to creating products or providing services, or to improving processes, the more efficient and effective the supply channel becomes. The better the supply system, the more wants and needs are met, the greater the potential for profit.

The complex system evident in the physical world is managed, manipulated, controlled by a force outside the physical world - infinite intelligence. You both have access to this force and are one with its substance.

We often think of money as a store of value, but the truth is, human beings store value.

With and within human beings reside both demand and the knowledge, know-how, and labor to provide the supply. These elements separately, or when combined with physical resources determine the nature, intent and outcome of market activities.

Human beings have monetary value; human beings don't drive the economy, human beings *are* the economy. Human beings possess a monetary value that in aggregate dwarfs the estimated value of all stuff. The power and potential of human beings is awesome.

People's ability, individually and collectively, to create is unlimited. The economy of the world, while by no means perfect, is evidence of human being's ability to desire, cooperate, and create.

People need and want products and services to survive. These aspects of the physical world add to our ability to feel. People also create - that is produce products and services to fulfill demand. Producing and creating are feeling acts. People are the economic engine, the economic fuel, and the economic drivers determining both supply and demand. We desire to enjoy the fruits of creation. We create, we consume, and in both we feel. Life is a magical adventure.

People make money, earn money, empower money. People are the makers and mistresses of markets. If you intend to create, give and receive. If you intend to amass a fortune, seek to understand and satisfy people, for they are the key to understanding money and markets - politics and economics. People desire, people create - people, not money, make the world go round.

ECONOMICS OF BELIEFS

Your *belief* about lack or scarcity is the most important determinant of whether or not you will ever become wealthy or you will ever accumulate property and possessions. Your beliefs are more important than knowledge, abilities or status. To paraphrase Henry Ford, "If you think you can be wealthy or you think you can't - you are right."

Where the average person sees lack, the achiever sees opportunity.

This notion of lack, and some foibles applying economic theory, may be the reasons economics has been labeled the dismal science. People have experienced

7: Money Politics and Economics

great pain, emotional and physical, due to market miscalculations. And, as seems to be common practice - the first order of business when something goes wrong is to find someone to blame - in our modern world economists are the usual suspects.

It's been said of economists, "If you laid all the economists in the world end to end, they would never reach a conclusion." "Economists are people who work with numbers but don't have the personality to be accountants." "An economist is someone who sees something work in practice and wonders if it would work in theory." And, "Give me a one-handed economist! Economists always say, 'On the one hand; on the other.'" The thrust of such criticism usually follows a market failure.

Economics looks to measure, qualify, quantify and explain the means and management of production and consumption. It attempts, through a methodical and systematic process to answer weighty questions related to human prosperity. Economists struggle to clearly define what happens in markets and why. Armed with the ammunition of learned economic theories, policy makers, capitalists, and entrepreneurs all try to leverage market insights to achieve profitable results. Those attempting to leverage economic insights however, fail to factor in the one variable that really matters. Economics has failed to quantify the intangible, the power of beliefs.

Theoretically people are rational, self-serving, interested in maximizing benefits and minimizing costs. Why then, can't economists formulate a market equation that determines accurately the economic response to a given stimuli? Because they are not considering all the factors in play. The economists' views are incomplete.

Economics is art and science attempting to explain cause and effect. Economists see what happened, label it, and then ascribe cause to the effect. What they misunderstand is that cause is not in the same dimension as effect. Expressed another way, economists seek to understand the world by drawing conclusions about cause only from effects - without really understanding cause.

The main driver of cause is *beliefs* - beliefs people have about who they are, what they can do, and the circumstances of this world. Adam Smith wrote in *The Wealth of Nations* of the "invisible hand" guiding markets, producing a collective benefit from the interaction of myriad self-interests. This invisible hand is in the realm of cause. The invisible hand is the force of motives, desires - belief.

Markets rise and fall, economies and societies are built, and individuals succeed or fail, as a result of human psyches - the application of energy by the mind, in the material world. Beliefs about abundance and scarcity, opportunities and limitations, impel individual prospects, which in turn empower collective progress. Economics seeks to make sense of a reality designed and moved by fundamental values and ideas about the world and society - the influence of spirit. The equation of supply and demand is less about capital, resources and systems, than it is about the condition of the human psyche, the mind in relation to spirit - to divine intelligence.

If people, not money, make the world go round, then it is *belief* about money, markets and exchange that is the energy moving the economy.

Don't make the economists' mistake; don't underestimate the influence of beliefs in markets or in life. What you believe creates your reality. If you believe in abundance you will prosper. If you subscribe to limitations boundaries will define your life. The most powerful economic theory is the one that rouses people to believe reality is limitless, resources are plentiful, and opportunities abound. Believe you can be wealthy, cling tight to that belief, and you will be wealthy. For beliefs drive economics.

AMBITIOUS - NOT ANY ROAD WILL DO

We esteem grit and determination, celebrate fortune and honor the victorious, yet we deride an ugly twist of fate. To provide relief we often go so far as to divorce the individual from culpability for negative happenings or states of affairs. By this thinking, if another or some force beyond control is responsible for the pain and suffering in that individual's life, might I not be responsible for the pain and suffering in mine?

Achievement and success go hand in hand with responsibility. The individual who succeeds must be willing to advance - must be willing to move forward along the journey of life.

For those without ambition, any detour, any delay, any road will do. People without ambition can afford to judge others, condemn and criticize. These people elevate being a victim to an art form. Indulging in these pursuits slows their pace and derails progress. As those without ambition don't care where they are headed, or when they will arrive, wading through trials is par for the course.

For those with ambition, however, detours are a delay; not any road will do. For those with a destination in mind, the route matters.

Your navigational aid in life is your ability to feel. Your selection of experiences is through your thoughts and your ability to choose. You get experiences that reflect what you give. So give good feelings and you'll guide yourself along the right route. While the big picture and even the subtle nuances of the environment may be beyond the individual, it is the choices people make, producing the feelings that they feel, that most directly influence the circumstances and the quality of the journey.

While you may not be able to choose the strength or the direction of the prevailing wind, you can choose to hoist, set, or strike your sails. You choose how you address the wind. You have at your disposal assets to leverage, both seen and unseen. The course and pace of the journey are up to you. No matter the proximity to your destination, recognize it is joy in the adventure that matters. Choose a course to make others feel good and you will feel good. The strength of your ambition and the choices you make negotiating the obstacles along the way determine the success not only in your life, but of your life.

The road before you is paved with choices. The choices are often not easy or free of pain. Few people are born to wealth and privilege, and many face daunting challenges. You can expect to endure hardship and suffer losses, but count your blessings; challenges build character. In your struggle you have opportunities to feel. And "to feel" is why you are here. Despite humble beginnings and persistent obstacles, realize you are meant to succeed in this life. You are here to fulfill a divine purpose. You have the tools at hand and the help you need standing by to achieve your purpose.

Exercise your will to choose. Choose a worthy destination. Pursue your greatest ambition and persevere in your choices to experience an extraordinary journey. The events of life, taken together, form a grand mosaic. Your contribution to this mosaic is time well spent, energy well invested. It is a legacy of good feelings you felt - feelings you shared.

Success is not a life of comfort or indecision and fear. Rather success is marked by ambition, by trials and triumph. Each event, for its part, is shaped by a small decision to act - to proceed. Each event, each twist and turn on the road is an opportunity for a thoughtful choice. Choose wisely, for the ambitious not any road will do.

YOUR CHOICE: POVERTY OR PROSPERITY?

Recognizing that all achievement begins with thought, people are often left to ask: "What was I thinking?"

When setting ourselves on the course to ruin, the best we can muster is to shuffle deck chairs. By refusing to confront the brutal facts we continue to reinforce the gravest of errors: trusting our lives, our fortunes, and our sacred honor to "powers that be - the powers of this world," and to chance, to fate, and to the whims of others.

It is time to choose again.

You have arrived. You are where you are now. While supported by a guiding hand, you chose the route, you finely tuned the vehicle, and you manipulated the path. If you chose poorly, don't attempt to rid yourself of a nagging sense of responsibility - embrace it and get going. People, by nature, seek absolute control over their lives. Power is, in fact, a birthright of every human being. Each person controls the direction, the speed and the experiences of their journey - for better or for worse. Each gets to choose. However, as people mature and come to understand the truth, they realize, along with ultimate power comes ultimate responsibility.

For far too many "responsibility" is a burden too cumbersome to bear. In haste to shed the yoke of responsibility people unwittingly forfeit power - they give it to other people. Because the ride of life intimidates and overwhelms, instead of claiming responsibility and charting a course, we unwittingly surrender power. This act, engaged in by enough people, allows a few to flourish at the expense of the many.

This process of abandoning responsibility and abdicating power has slowly but surely concentrated power in the hands of the few. The powerful are the people, capable or not, honorable or not, who are willing to wield power. These are the ones to whom we entrust our lives. In relinquishing power we submit a feeble petition, "take care of us." We surrender the promise and potential of a grand adventure for a groundless guarantee of a measure of comfort and an illusion of security. For we "are more disposed to suffer, while evils are sufferable, than to right..." ourselves with purity of thought, effort, and ingenuity.

We console ourselves believing, the men of great wealth and industry possess wisdom. They know best and will provide adequately for our needs. We give our trust, mistakenly convincing ourselves of the empty promises of empowered elites. Those who gladly take the power we confer. Feigning helplessness, we expect the captains of industry and the titans of finance to benevolently create ever greater wealth while we glow in the light of their brilliance.

We expect a faceless bureaucracy to care for the needs of the many - while the system we created and reinforce diverts the bounty into the hands of the few. We seed power eagerly to those willing to exercise it, believing naively, they have our best interests at heart.

But what of the alternative?

If we were to accept total responsibility for our lives and our choices, who would we blame? Who could we convict? Who can we condemn?

There is no one to blame.

To reclaim your birthright, you must have vision, commit to a direction, and summon the courage and fortitude to proceed. Resolve to discipline yourself, to shepherd our own journey - to choose the best path. To right your course you must accept total responsibility for what you have created.

The trials and tribulations we see in politics are the result of the people, "we the people," abdicating power and forsaking responsibility. The power to correct this error lies with each individual - it lies with you.

ECONOMICS IS NOT ALL ABOUT PROFIT

America is locked in a relentless struggle against a toxic, pervasive idea. The idea infects seemingly thoughtful, intelligent individuals, ultimately setting those people and their organizations on a course to self-destruct.

From boardroom to boardroom and business school to business school the contagion spreads. Influential people mistakenly buy into a caustic notion - a lie that at once undermines social trust, corrupts democratic politics, and destroys faith in free enterprise on an industrial scale. The ultimate boardroom lie: "Business exists for profit." When the truth is, the economy is not first and foremost about generating profit.

The word "profit" as used here requires a fine distinction. Profit is not meant as a desire for mutual benefit or growth. It is not something altruistic or selfless. No, profit means revenue, return, income.

The mistaken belief is that the purpose of trade is to achieve unilateral gain or selfish advantage - to make money, pure and simple. From this perspective, if it weren't for a few socially imposed rules, commerce might just as well be crime. In a cutthroat society where economic ends (profit) justify means, everyone pays a price.

Symptoms of this intellectual infection are rampant. Look no further then the shenanigans of the financial industry and the folly of Wall Street; or the seemingly endless stream of nickel and dime charges and fees proposed by multinational behemoths to drain customers at every turn.

Leadership in American industry has increasingly succumbed to the notion that the prime objective of commerce is profit. Leaders suffering from this delusion worship first and foremost at the altar of profit. Instead of serving, instead of adding value, they seek to fleece the consumer and line their own pockets. They don't realize the scope of the negative consequences this bias imposes.

We recognize that every transaction requires two complicit actors. For one person to play the role of perpetrator, another must play the role of victim. To have people who would claim power, others must be willing to give it up. This dynamic of "corruption" is the consequence of people's desires and people's actions. We only have ourselves to blame for the dysfunction of the system.

A commercial enterprise springs from an idea to solve a problem, meet a need, add value. A productive enterprise (for profit, not for profit, or government) is the effort of an individual or group to create a response to a demand - a want or need. Profit is a byproduct of success in fulfilling needs and satisfying desires. Profit comes *after* giving - after generating value, after producing or providing something useful. Not before.

As a business grows and prospers, it establishes and nourishes trust. A prosperous organization fine-tunes its offerings and becomes more proficient, efficient and effective meeting needs and fulfilling desires. Eventually, however, all thriving organizations are challenged - by competition from without or corruption from within. If the organization's leadership focuses on the by-product (profit) instead of the inspiring purpose (creating value), the company is doomed.

In a reality bent on expansion, growth and increasing worth (life's purpose) - only individuals and organizations that add value survive and flourish. Fixating on profit accumulation is like punching the self-destruct button. Dissolution is only a matter of time. The misconception that business exists only for profit is fueled by a dangerous combination of insatiable desire (the natural human condition) and unconstrained opportunity. Here is where success is the seed of its own demise. Ego asserts itself in the most destructive way.

Without the moderating influence of a moral, collaborative social culture, competition and greed usurp the economic system. Without the moderating, positive influence of divine intelligence, the result is always a cataclysmic end. When ego is in charge any notion of mutual benefit, of adding value, flies out the window. If an organization does not add value - does not contribute to life - it will die. It's how life works.

In a healthy society, business is not about accumulating and amassing. Business is a mutually beneficial, culturally enhancing activity. Commerce helps people live well. The purpose of commerce, economic exchange, trade, is to add value - to solve problems - to meet needs. Commerce is a social compact, founded on common trust and collective self-interest. If a corporate board member, a business school professor, or a highly placed public official suggests business is primarily about profit, or is meant to earn a return for investors, suspicion is in order. Your moral fiber is about to be tested.

People espousing the profit motive as the chief aim of business or the basis for an economy fail to grasp the tenets of human relations, the bedrock foundation upon which free enterprise rests. They operate in the realm of effect, never recognizing the higher order of cause.

American business over the last century has achieved extraordinary results. The United States has prospered spectacularly because of a dogged determination to solve problems and satisfy desires. People have been driven by pure motives. The United States created prosperity by working in concert with the laws of nature - with divine intelligence. If America continues to propagate the ultimate boardroom lie, and attempts to work counter to the laws of nature - resisting divine intelligence - the future will not be so bright.

Don't propagate the lie. Don't let the infection spread. Focus on the right motive - to create value - in all business dealings - in every aspect of life. Choose the right path.

ALL FOR ONE HAS FAILED
ONE FOR ALL

Recall the *Three Musketeers* battle cry: "All for one and one for all"? Today our modern economic system serves half this axiom - "All for one." When the system falters, instead of working for the betterment of all - it begins to function enriching the few.

Our system is at full production concentrating wealth in unprecedented measure. As power shifts from the many to the few, "all" pay the price. The single greatest cause of the worldwide economic unraveling is our tendency to run away from responsibility. This results in our propensity for consolidating power and concentrating wealth. Because we fear the demands of responsibility, we tolerate a dysfunctional system. The "system" - economic and political - now functions to elevate a few at the expense of many.

When we find ourselves in the midst of challenging economic times all is not lost. Even in the Great Depression of the 1930s, the world kept spinning, the sun rose each day, men and women married, babies were born, people started businesses, fortunes were made - life went on. Those who focused on life's simple pleasures remained resilient and some even prospered. Faith in a brighter tomorrow carried the day - like it always does.

To move forward during difficult times, to recover, to prosper we, individually and collectively, must choose anew. We must expose the error of our ways and act purposely and deliberately knowing we, all of us, have the power to change this world now. By together choosing a new future, we usher in a new reality and we create a new experience.

The rich and powerful see the writing on the wall. They recognize and are poised to take advantage of human nature. When the opportunity avails itself and "the people" surrender their power and their freedom, the willing (those intent on wielding power) leverage the system. They attempt to secure wealth and power - ensuring both flow to their advantage.

Today we have a system that, unless fundamentally altered, will continue to disenfranchise the masses and in the end destroy itself. Now, as mentioned, the masses have created this monster. Eventually the people will reclaim their power. This concentration of power has once again proved the rule: "Power corrupts, and absolute power corrupts absolutely." Humanity will continue to experience this trial until we learn the lesson. We overlook the ultimate solution to this economic challenge because we are so engrossed in the problem we cannot or dare not, step back to seek and embrace real change. Fundamental change means assuming responsibility and reclaiming personal power.

Though we clamor for change, truly we fear it. We cling to the known - we trust in the state and the system to provide for our needs. We endure the discomfort we brought on ourselves, until, overcome by events, we are swept up by a tide - the tide of life - a tide of change. Life intends for us to grow, so in the end we must change.

The only thing people like better than the way things are is the way things were. Change is a difficult, scary thing, to powerless, insecure people.

We didn't arrive at this predicament over night. Neither Rome nor our economic system were built in a day. The forfeiting and consolidation of power has been occurring over generations. At the end of World War II, by necessity the United States stepped in to restore a shattered global economic system. As could be predicted, however, the arrogance of power gave way to the ingenuity of greed, and the all too human desire for comfort. We began to build a system serving the basest desires of the masses for comfort and security driven by those bold and brazen enough to compete for the prize of wealth and power.

We shifted from creating and cooperating, sharing and serving, to competing and contesting, hoarding and dominating - not just in America, but around the world. While most companies genuinely advanced principles of mutual benefit, many did not. When we failed to have faith in an ideal of growth - a dream of what could be - greed dictated we fight for the biggest share of what already existed.

America, the land of opportunity, was built on the power of dreams and the promise of prosperity to those with the courage to create. In the age of ascendency Americans took responsibility for themselves and found a way to add value to others' lives. Losing our sight, our vision, our dreams, we settle into the mud and mire of the struggle. Running from responsibility, we choose comfort and security over freedom and power. Scaling back our aspirations we sacrifice our freedom and we throw open the doors to those who seek to consolidate power.

People willingly forfeit their dreams for a sense of security and a modicum of comfort. Without pure motives the masses succumb to the allure of the powerful. Aggressive competitors seize opportunities and consolidate power. What we have been seeing and experiencing for the past sixty-five years is a methodical consolidation of power and wealth. This centralization of wealth and power led to the excesses, the greed and corruption, of the early 2000s debt bubble, which persists still. We made our bed and now lie in it.

To chart a new course we have to energize the many. Not through a welfare state, but by promoting fair, just free enterprise and sound social policies. Individuals must learn how life works and begin moving in the right direction. Change in economics, and change in politics happens one person, one decision at a time. One by one, as each person claims his or her power the world changes. As people willingly assume responsibility for their lives, they will wield the power to change reality - and reality will change.

Those who seek a new political and economic direction cannot continue centralizing wealth, but must rather work to empower people. This is done by claiming and exercising personal power. The goal must be for people to take responsibility for themselves and once again dream grand dreams. Then people can pursue splendid opportunities.

To achieve this goal for everyone, you must first achieve this end for you. If we continue to choose the status quo, we will decline as a nation and a culture. It is time to truly fulfill the axiom: "All for one, and one for all."

AMERICA'S WAY OUT OF THE STORM

Disheartening unemployment, unprecedented debt (personal, corporate and public), expensive foreign wars, an aging population, and polarized politics hardly represent America at its prime. Some contend America has reached its zenith and is on the waning side of the peak. We have been beaten and battered by choices made, public and private, and the folly we have collectively pursued. A small minority profit handsomely while the vast majority pays the fare. We remain caught in the storm - a storm of our own making.

We have harkened to the altar of Keynes and Friedman. We have pledged our sons and daughters to the blighted cause in far off lands. We have traded liberty for a false veil of security. We have exhausted every means to avoid paying the toll, yet the toll taker remains vigilant and steadfast - there is no free lunch. It is time to pay the price for our comfort and our complacency.

We now face the most difficult of choices: we can run, we can hide; we can attempt to salvage some scrap from the wreckage; or we can choose a most challenging path - a path through the storm. As was once affirmed: "It is better to meet danger than to wait for it. He that is on a lee shore, and foresees a hurricane, stands out to sea and encounters a storm to avoid a wreck." America's way out of the storm is through it.

The greatness of America was not that of empire, not that of a domineering oppressor, but rather the product of a feisty counterpuncher - an underdog. America's prowess was built on an adventurous spirit where the height of one's accomplishment rested on the breadth of one's character. A sentiment of fairness and equality served as the foundation, however imperfectly, for concerted effort, unconstrained creativity, and uncompromising collaboration.

America, a land of immigrants, at its best was a community of communities. Newcomers ventured to the promised land not in search of a handout and gilded bed-rest but rather to take advantage of a hand up and put themselves to the test in pursuit of the grandest of dreams. Americans aimed high, risked everything, set colossal goals, and applied their blood, sweat and tears to forge new paths through the wilderness, build vast, life-affirming organizations, leverage unprecedented resources, and best any threat to their autonomy. American assets were the capital of free enterprise tempered by a hardened conviction to succeed.

The American dream was not a welfare state - the condition of individuals living off a nameless, faceless, patronizing bureaucracy. America was a land of the people, by the people, for the people. This land of rugged individualists achieved preeminence by way of unparalleled cooperation and unforeseen good fortune brought on by a willingness to dream big and risk it all. The American experience was a test of a free people to apply themselves as they saw fit. Together they gave, they took, they worked, they laughed, they cried, they shared, they overcame.

The storm upon America now is the result of the disintegration of that collaborative spirit. Since the United States has risen to supremacy, its beacon has faded. We have succumbed to the allure of power - where power corrupts and absolute power corrupts absolutely. We have set ourselves on a course to centralize wealth in the hands of the moneyed elite and rest the vestiges of political control from the disenchanted and deliberately isolated masses placing power squarely into the hands of the politically privileged.

The way out of the storm now is to decentralize. We must return the power to the people, to community. Those with legitimate interests must regain control. As the artist Vincent Van Gogh once observed, "Fishermen know that the sea is dangerous and the storm terrible, but they have never found these dangers sufficient reason for remaining ashore." It is time for the electorate to reclaim America. We change the world by changing ourselves.

The moneyed interests and political apparatus seek only to appease voters, promising ever greater prosperity while ensuring ever more tumultuous times. To the powerful the storm never surges as they have erected barriers - the weak, ill-informed and malleable masses. The means for individuals and society to weather this storm is to overcome the ego - abandon competition - for renewed collaboration. We cannot reclaim the American dream by competing for ever-diminishing pieces of pie. We must create a bigger pie individually and together.

Apply a litmus test to every business or political proposal, knowing the only way out is to pay the bill. Does the proposal require commitment, sacrifice, vision by the people, for the people? If the offering does not, the scheme is likely snake oil designed to disadvantage the many for the benefit of the few. Only community will prevail in this storm. We are in this together, we must take control and cooperate with one another to navigate our way out.

The ultimate purpose of life is to relate and create - to feel. Our egos have led us into this malaise of competition and accumulation. America still has untapped resources of ingenuity, labor, physical assets and, if it can be invoked once again, undaunted fortitude. We need only the will to act and the foresight to once again dream great dreams - not for personal aggrandizement but for the betterment of all mankind. You see, it is not that this storm is only affecting America - the world is embroiled in the tumult. The world needs a beacon of hope.

Is America willing to once again assume that mantle? Once an ideal of opportunity and achievement, America can again find its way. We must collectively and cooperatively stop the madness. For by seeing a vision and committing to a cause greater than our selves we can regain our footing. America's way out of the storm is through it. The shared sacrifice of the people, for the people, can and will carry the day. Are you up to the challenge?

UNCOMMON SENSE

At a turning point in American history, a time of conflict where citizens had by necessity to choose sides, Thomas Paine affirmed: "These are the times that try men's souls. The summer soldier and the sunshine patriot will, in this crisis, shrink from the service of their country; but he that stands by it now, deserves the love and thanks of man and woman. Tyranny, like hell, is not easily conquered; yet we have this consolation with us, that the harder the conflict, the more glorious the triumph. What we obtain too cheap, we esteem too lightly: it is dearness only that gives every thing its value."

Freedom was the celestial condition for which Thomas Paine yearned. The bulwark of freedom was the foundation upon which lives of substance, lives of meaning, lives of opportunity were to be built. Only by charting one's own course are human beings truly alive.

The vestiges of oppression can never fulfill a dream of prosperity or peace or happiness. While a sovereign or omnipotent state might maintain a level of civility and order, without freedom the individual never matures. The individual never assumes full responsibility for his or her contributions, his or her accomplishments, his or her journey of life. By collaborating for the common good mankind rises from a subsistence existence to fulfill a destiny ordained by providence. This notion was nothing but common sense in 1776; but it is an idea seemingly lost on contemporary generations.

Over two hundred years after Thomas Paine exhorted his fellow colonists to stand against tyranny and oppression, Americans self-righteously console themselves as the beacon of freedom for a troubled world. Yet despite delusions of grandeur America wallows aimlessly on the precipice of calamity. Once the greatest creditor nation on earth, the United States is now the greatest debtor nation the world has ever known. The weakness of the masses and the collusion of titans of finance, captains of industry, and the puppeteers of politics have eroded a once noble foundation.

While the people seek aggressively to yield power, the elite work feverishly to consolidate and amass gains. The huddled masses, seeking comfort and security are placated with bread and games. The promise of freedom - to realize prosperity and comfort (the ends) - has been achieved. Unfortunately, current generations believe the prosperity others earned is a birthright for them to enjoy. This attitude of privilege has replaced a propensity for action, a willingness to shoulder burdens, and the courage to assume responsibility (the means). The cart is before the horse.

Collaboration to build a brighter future for successive generations, has deteriorated into a no-holds barred competition for the crumbs falling from banquet tables. Collective self-interest - to cooperate, collaborate, work and succeed - has been replaced by avarice and scheming, competition and corruption. Moral clarity - striving for justice, tranquility and the general welfare - have been usurped by the drive to consume, control and dominate. We have lost our way.

Concentrating wealth, and the power attendant in wealth, is the one existential threat to the greatest experiment in self-governance ever contrived. We the people, all of us, are complicit in this derision. As in all places and times, oppressors and the oppressed are co-conspirators. Fear and greed are the instruments of manipulation to which the masses fall victim. As it is "the people's government," the people are responsible for the travesties committed. The people have, measure by measure, supported the wearing away of principled, disciplined governance. Through the system the people refined, we have allowed the frailties of human nature to flourish, consummating in a leaderless coup. Failing to stand together, we fall apart. The means of affluence flow to ever more emboldened hands.

Now is the moment to apply uncommon sense. To regain our footing we must return to our roots. By the ingenuity of mind, conviction of spirit and sweat of the brow America prospered. But in celebrating success earned by prior generations we have grown satiated, satisfied and comfortable. Our penchant for consumption ushers in ruin. The uncommon sense, "in these times that try men's souls," is to discipline ourselves, rein ourselves in, sacrifice and endure the pain. "What we obtain too cheap, we esteem too lightly." The days of the American global empire are passed. We must make the hard choices to restore fiscal discipline. We must clip the wings of gluttonous opportunists.

Righting our course demands uncommon measures by a free and noble people. "The harder the conflict, the more glorious the triumph." Let us not fade from this task. The government of the United States was established as an experiment of sorts, on the capacity of mankind for self-government. The intent was that a free people, could, should and ought to govern themselves. To manage and promote the growth of a nation, the founding fathers created a democratic republic. They affirmed the notion that government was beholden to the people and that it had no other source of power.

Critics abound, attacking, for good reason, virtually every aspect of the U.S. system of governance. Ours is a system intentionally designed to reach compromise slowly and uneasily. The system is designed on this premise: the less government, the better. We recognize plenty of problems in government. The faults can easily be placed on the "system," but remember, the system is made up of people. Our experiment is one of collective self-government. It is the motives of the people collectively that determine the validity and vitality of the system.

The fault in self-government lies less with the *government* and more with the *self*. To improve the system, individuals must change. We must understand how life works, and work with life. To get something better, we have to give something better. Economics and politics are a reflection of the people - the individuals - that comprise the system. When we rise to our highest potential, the system rises with us. The material world responds to our hearts desires. We, you and I, can do better.

We change our lives by the choices we make. We change the world by the choices we make. Politics and economics are effects of those choices.

7: Money Politics and Economics

Success 101: How Life Works

8
THE NEXT STEP

So, here we are.

Just like the flood of images people report when facing death, life is flashing by. You are moving, everything is moving, life is moving. You are on a journey. You travel a road; or as by way of an even better metaphor: you are being carried down a river - the river of life. The river will not stop flowing; the clock will not stop ticking; you will not stop moving. So why not make the most of it?

Prospects are passing you by. More opportunities and options are fast approaching. The power to choose is yours. The responsibility to choose is yours. Your choices determine both your actions and the creations you will encounter. Your choices amount to the life you experience. You create your own reality.

You create your reality through your choices - the thoughts you entertain and the feelings you generate. You are the magician. You make the magic. Create the magic. Move in the right direction - enthusiastically, fearlessly. Take the next step in the right direction.

As we draw to a close, I will once again beat the drum. I hope and pray the rhythm of repetition serves you well...

SEEK TO FIND

A journey of a thousand miles begins with you...

You are a spiritual being vested in a body, experiencing perspectives of this reality, taking it all in. You have tools available to navigate the sea of change. And that is precisely what this life is, a sea of change. All is in motion. Your progression through time and space is a journey. You travel to explore and experience, to give and to grow. You can choose to be passenger or driver, the journey begins and ends with that choice.

A journey of a thousand miles begins with one small step - your step. The journey begins with you. You live literally and figuratively in the moment - *now*. There exists no other time. The past is memory, the future a dream. The moment is framed by the past and future; now is a bridge between the two. You never leave the bridge. Life happens on the bridge.

You can remember the past or, through a gift (some say a curse) of imagining, envision a future, but try as you might, you cannot escape the experience of now. This is a rule of the game. You are always at the synapse, the juncture point of energy in transition. You are on a journey from here to there. This journey is the flow of energy through your perception.

Enlightenment is the realization that you are master of the experience. Your interpretations of what you perceive creates the energy you experience. Seeking is desire moved into action.

To change direction, seek.

To achieve a new result, seek.

To find your heart's desire, seek.

Among the navigation tools available to you are: intellect (the radio tuner to ideas and memories), emotions, feelings, and the physical capacity to move through time and space. These tools allow you, if you so choose, to change perspective.

Even with the vast potential of life, some people squander their energy and fritter away their time trying to resist change. They would rather maintain things the way they are, or they pine for things as they were. Resisting change is ultimately a futile effort. Life is always and forever on the move. You might as well move ahead.

You are a being, a localized essence of awareness, in a particular time and space, experiencing a wondrous reality. At the same time you are, to a degree, swept up by the environment surrounding you. The opportunity life offers lies in employing your tools, setting your sails and navigating the sea of change to create anew. You get to choose your experience, the route of your journey, the limits of your adventure. Desire is your catalyst for change. Maintain a positive focus and you will be amazed at the astonishing experiences that come into your awareness. Seek to find a full and fulfilling life.

LET GO, STOP RESISTING

Do you ever just feel stuck?

Is life, your life not all you had hoped?

Are you struggling personally? Professionally?

Is life moving fast? Too fast?

Are you having trouble finding your way?

Are you facing a crisis?

You have probably heard: "Buried in every crisis is opportunity." Are you looking for an opportunity now? Any opportunity? Just some relief?

Well, stop searching. There is an easier way.

Challenges, obstacles help us stretch and learn and grow. Every challenge, large or small, has a means to overcome evident in it (sometimes not so evident - but there still, nonetheless). What you need to surmount any and every obstacle you encounter (or create) is always available. Unfortunately, sometimes we are overwhelmed by what we encounter; sometimes we get swept up in the storm.

When facing overwhelming odds our natural human inclination is to hold on tight. We dig in. We cling. We resist the forces of change. We batten down the hatches in a storm. We attempt to defy the wind. We cling to the rocks in rushing rapids. We focus all our energy on beating back the threat when the real solution, the essential key is to let go.

The way to realize the promise of life - to fulfill your potential - is to stop putting up a fight. Stop resisting. Life is a kaleidoscope of change. This reality is energy in motion. Obstacles come and go, they flow together and they subside. Your resistance, your clinging holds obstacles in place. By focusing on the obstacle you lose sight of your goal, your aim, your purpose. When you continue to face an obstacle you freeze your own motion. As long as you resist you slow down time - the threat stays with you, because you stay with it. The only requirement to succeed, to change the circumstances of your life, is a willingness to move on.

When you fall victim to the desire, or the need, or the fear, to cling to current circumstances you are resisting the force of change - you are resisting life itself. The means to prevail over any obstacle is always present. The energy, the strength, is available to the extent of your capacity to change, to journey on, to grow. The path of least resistance is to dissolve obstacles, reduce challenges, eliminate adversity by going with the flow. You need not be a solitary force against the world. You are here, in this reality, with a means, a capacity to navigate - a facility to move and unlimited assistance. You can linger and struggle or you can move on and create. The choice is yours. Everything is in motion - join the dance.

This reality is perpetual change. The collage is constantly reshaping itself into intricate, complex patterns and simple, beautiful designs. Sometimes the pattern forms obstacles - sometimes bridges. On this ride of your life, navigate past the obstacles; cross the bridges - go with the flow. The purpose for your being may not be evident; it may not be plain, yet you are here - you are on the journey. You have at your command a wellspring of power - the energy of a universe in motion - move with it. Stop resisting - let go!

CHANGE YOUR LIFE NOW

In pain - lost in a troubling abyss, or just nursing a feeling of discontent about your place in this world - know, without a doubt, you can in fact change your life. You can start anew. The path is not invisible, the puzzle is not unsolvable, the truth not unknowable. If you want to head in a new direction, experience a new life and embrace a new reality, think and act anew. Now can be your moment of change.

Start from where you are. Find the answers within. Judge not, nor affix blame. To release the bonds that bind you - forgive. Self-righteous condemnation only imprisons you. Accept responsibility to change what you can - yourself.

> Let go of ego (the need to control) and the fear ego employs.

> To grow - love unconditionally and live with abandon. Life is intended to be a journey of joy.

Master the Half Dozen for Success:
1. Live each moment.

2. Listen to the still, small voice within.

3. Control self (accept, let go, forgive) - master ego.

4. Overcome fear.

5. Act on faith.

6. Stay the course.

To experience a full and fulfilling life: live wisely, act courageously, rely on your inner strength and by your will persevere. There are forces beyond your knowing looking out for you.

Seems easy enough, doesn't it?

Implement simple measures to transform your life. To live each moment, focus on the here and now. Accept the circumstances you face as having come from who you were. Reserve judgment - instead become someone new. Your circumstances will change. To find the truth within, reflect before acting. Don't let the power of emotion sweep you into bondage. Replace bad feelings with good feelings and you'll get more good feelings.

Pray, meditate, center yourself and listen. The still, small voice may be but a faint whisper. With consistent attention, you will find that voice and it will point you in the right direction.

Don't try to eliminate fear. Instead eliminate fear's power over you. Observe fear. Feel its influence. Embrace and accept that energy in your body. Come to recognize that "feeling" of apprehension and empower yourself to act despite fear.

Life is a journey, a quest, an adventure. To direct your voyage - act. Take the next step on faith. For death approaches when you stop moving forward. Discipline of will allows you to persevere. Life cannot and will not defeat you, so long as you never give up. When life seems overwhelming and circumstances impossible to overcome, remember - you have been given other people, challenges, and a universe of opportunity so as not to become self-absorbed - trapped by ego. Help yourself by helping others.

Master thought, focus your mind. All things are possible. Change your life. One life - your life - well lived, changes the world.

CHOOSE WHAT WILL BE

As both creation and creator you have an extraordinary opportunity in this reality - this earthly playground. Your mission is to fulfill the promise and potential of life.

Grounded in an immense landscape, you are an actor in an epic tale written across generations. You are meant to contribute a unique and vital element to this heroic, romantic adventure. Without your contribution the story is incomplete. You possess a distinct and powerful gift with which to make your mark. You have the ability to choose. You can choose what you will do, what you will be and, to a degree, what will be. Though it may not seem that way when you are lost in the illusion, the rules of the game are stacked in your favor. The outcome is pre-determined. In the end you will arrive at a glorious destination. Only the route is left to determine - you get to choose the path.

When you are disoriented and overwhelmed, then you experience conflict and strife - disharmony and discord. Interpretations of discontent are burdens you lay on yourself. Instead of letting go of painful circumstances you hold tightly to what you know. Instead of observing and accepting, you judge. Instead of allowing what will be, to be, you seek reassurance and demand control. Contradictions are rampant in this existence. You observe contrast but often fail to see meaning, purpose, harmony, unity. The tides of change ebb and flow with a rhythmic persistence yet, somehow, you find yourself adrift, lost at sea. Imprisoned by "human" nature, caught in the emotion of being, you succumb to ego and fall victim to fear. The need to survive, the energy of emotion, and the limitations of the intellect are overwhelmed by a complex environment, the demands of the moment, and the challenges of the flesh. Embracing the "world" view, you forget your "true" nature and mistakenly put stock in the notion, "It's me against the world." This need not be the reality you embrace.

You are on a journey from the trifles of everyday existence to the exuberance of ultimate joy. Wisdom is realizing the truth: you are whole, complete, timeless and immortal. You are spirit on a human journey. You are an observer of a vast illusion - an illusion at once rich in texture and diversity, alive and dynamic and yet simple and elegant and graceful. The illusion is awe inspiring and profoundly uplifting. You will journey to where you are meant to be. Don't waste your life on a troubling route. Face the unknown with trust and faith.

Choose not to be lost in the illusion. Choose another way. Choose rightly and persevere in your choice until the smoke clears, the fog lifts, the clouds part - until the truth reveals itself. Instead of choosing to experience pain and loss and fear, choose again - choose until you find the joy that awaits - choose what will be.

HAVE LIFE MORE ABUNDANTLY

Our understanding of this life colors the reality we experience. These are our beliefs.

Most of humanity binds itself into the drudgery of an isolated, perilous existence - an existence grounded in the known - an existence of sight and sound and feeling. We believe we have limits. We believe we are powerless. The often-misunderstood truth is that our boundaries are not static or fixed; home is not here, and we can go home. Something outside physical reality exists. A power, beyond our own, organizes and animates what we experience.

When we limit ourselves we follow a script of scarcity, a script of sacrifice, a script of desperation. Conflict, challenge, and effort are component parts of the drama lending depth, texture, and context, a credibility the ego demands. But we need not revel in the drama; we have a choice, and we can choose another way.

Life is infinitely more than the limited physical reality we readily accept. Understanding that another reality exists is beyond intellect, in the realm of faith. Faith in an ultimate truth requires a willingness to move beyond intellect to be open to a truth that seeks to reveal itself. Our very existence, our awareness of life and this physical reality, is like a dream. Yet buried in the dream is a gift, a promise already granted - we need only accept it. The promise is one of opportunity and adventure, risk nestled in security.

We are like children learning to ride a bike. We are scared and exhilarated at the same time, but still under the guiding hand of a loving parent. The power that animates and energizes this physical reality offers alternatives. We have unlimited resources and vast potential to draw on to discover and create in this playground. We have the power to choose. To discover the truth you must choose to follow the guide leading you home.

You have a guide. That still, small voice that whispers to you in times of trouble, that implores you to turn at times of decision, that seeks your happiness in a sometimes sullen world, is the force showing you the way.

The examples of sages and saints guide us to doorways of spirit - each person must go through. Choose to be open to the promise and potential of an unlimited life of peace, love, and joy. Do not succumb to the weight of the drama. The promise is a life of unlimited potential. Orient on the promise and potential of life and you will have life more abundantly.

WHAT IS YOUR NEW AIM IN LIFE?

Are you where you want to be?

> Are you as accomplished as you had hoped to be at this point in your life?
>
> Are you pushing beyond your comfort zone?
>
> Are you striving valiantly and giving generously?
>
> Are you more than contributing and earning all you are worth?
>
> Are you achieving your goals?
>
> Are you taking time for yourself?
>
> Are you surrounded by people that love and support you?
>
> Are you realizing your potential?
>
> In short, are you living a full and fulfilling life?

If the answer to any one, or all of these questions is no, the first thing to recognize is life has no time for regrets. There are no "do-overs." Life is a one-way trip. You can only move forward. There is no going back.

It is helpful to know where you are, but it is crucially important, critical, essential, to know where you are going. What is your aim in life?

You possess unlimited potential. You are programmed for success. You are a success magnet. You in fact, succeed at everything you try. That is, you get, from all your attempts, an opportunity to experience, to become, to grow. This is a truth of life. Your purpose for being in this time and in this place is to experience; to ride the ride; to be and become. In life you are meant to grow to your ultimate potential, and by so doing you fulfill your purpose for taking on a human form.

Now you, like most people, can take life as it comes. You can stumble through it. You can create by accident. You can muddle from one mediocre circumstance to another. You can try this or try that. You can venture left or right, or keep circling around. You can even sit down and resist the urge to go and to grow. The choice is yours. The time horizon on the scale of eternity is endless, but your opportunity now - that chance before you - is finite.

In the life you are leading (and make no mistake, you are leading), you get to choose. If you choose correctly you can be and become much, much more.

What you experience today, the circumstances you find yourself in, were brought to you by what you focused on, what you thought about, in the preceding series of yesterdays. Your life (as is every life) is the sum product of your own creation. You form, fashion and craft the circumstances you encounter. You bring what you intend into your experience. You have, in your possession, the ultimate weapon. You possess the power. You enjoy absolute control. Your thoughts create your life. Be careful what you aim for.

Your passage through this life can be a haphazard journey of fits and starts, trials and tribulations, or it can be an exhilarating adventure. The difference between an awe-inspiring life of thrills and one of drudgery and fear is determined by your focus, your attention, your aim. What matters in life is that you aim well and that you move toward your target. If you choose properly and you persist, no obstacle will stop you, no condition will defeat you, no attempt will ever constitute failure. The power of the universe is with you. Aim for something worthwhile and get moving.

The radiance of a meaningful goal will cast off all shadows. Joy is in the journey. Engage your time, your talents, and your emotion in an aim that energizes you, that empowers you, that fulfills you. For then you will have chosen to create a life of significance. Aim well.

LIFE'S AMUSEMENT PARK

This journey of life is like a merry-go-round, a rollercoaster, a waterslide. You pick the thrill ride. Amusement park rides are a combination of foreboding, anticipation, sheer terror and exhilaration. The reason people love these rides so much is that they bring out intense feelings, emotions and sensations rarely experienced in the everyday humdrum.

Even the merry-go-round, often a child's first introduction to the sights, sounds, and sensations of an amusement park, still elicit fond feelings of nostalgia and glee for harried adults who, having long ago abandoned the fantasy of the stampede, cling to tender memories of faded youth.

Hardly an adult thrill ride the merry-go-round still pleases. Have you ever watched a young child approach the merry-go-round for his or her first ride? The children watch on the sidelines mesmerized and enchanted by the glitz of galloping horses and pulsing of tinny music. Some want to clamor on board from the first instant they absorb the energy. Others, more reserved and cautious, must work up their courage before joining in the fun.

What is, or has been your approach to life? Are you inclined to jump right in? Do you prefer the rollercoaster over the merry-go-round? Or are you idling on the sidelines - waiting for everything to be just right - waiting to be sure it's safe? Life beckons you to throw caution to the wind.

Anxious children, impatient for their parents to purchase tickets, can't wait for the gate to release them for the merry-go-round. The impetuous scramble aboard the platform and rush for the grandest beast they can find. Towering above the young child, the biggest mechanical creatures perch at the apex of their stride - far too high for a small child to mount. To the determined youngster, however, the height is just one minor obstacle to overcome, like so many in their immature lives. They persevere for the utter delight of the ride.

This is how life is meant to be.

For a more reserved child, the merry-go-round elicits some trepidation. Observed from a distance, the safety of the gallery, the merry-go-round offers the hint of a thrill. From the observer's point of view, the riders seem to be having fun. But still, the speed, the size, the noise - all seem threatening. Maybe, in just the right spot - in one of the carriages, or possibly on a horse that doesn't gallop, but rather coasts along - this child can enjoy the fun. Just maybe the young child can push fear aside, and for a few minutes blend with the rhythm of the ride, the flash of the lights, the beat of the music, and let themselves go.

Going somewhere is better than standing still. Joining with the rhythm of life beats resisting its flow.

The merry-go-round, the roller coaster, the tilt-a-whirl, all amusement park rides leverage the same forces - gravity and acceleration. These forces produce rarely felt sensations that amount to seldom expressed emotions - thrills. On these rides people experience fits and jolts, twists and turns, catapulted ascents and gut-wrenching drops, all from a position of relative safety. Though the experience is controlled and artificial, the sensations are real.

The speed, the power and the motion of amusement park rides arouse excitement people both long for and fear in everyday life, if only for a few moments. The real world is just the same. The warfare and diplomacy of politics and the hustle and bustle of business, of seeking and providing goods and services, are their own types of rides. Better these activities produce good feelings (sensations the riders enjoy) than bad (sensations the riders dread).

Unlike amusement park rides, however, politics and economics are life processes that don't stop. You can't get on and get off, get in and get out, when you're ready. Power is a dynamic function of life. Material needs are a component of this journey. Life is moving, you are advancing or retreating by the choices you make - the intentions you nurture.

Like the amusement park rides, though, the ride of your life offers plenty of opportunity for chills and thrills, highs and lows, ups and down. All of it - life - is one sweet ride. Get in on it.

WHO CONTROLS THE RIDE?

The beauty of an amusement park ride is that you can enjoy with abandon. The rider knows she is safe, knows the experience is temporary, knows the result - good or bad - will be fleeting. To enjoy the ride, people give up control.

What about the ride of life? Who controls this ride?

When considering the ride of life, though most people would concede maintaining absolute control is not realistic; the desire and the initial reaction is typically "I want to be in control." But can you be on the ride, in the experience, in the moment, and at the controls too?

We know there are two immutable limits on what we can control in our lives. We do not knowingly control the circumstances of our birth. And we do not consciously control the limits of our human life. We know that someday each of us, like every person who has gone before, will die. We transitioned into life, we will transition out. Over these two things, birth and death, no person has control. We awaken as if from a dream to find ourselves on an amusement park ride, a ride we often believe is not of our choosing. And with the acquisition of some life experience we come to realize that the ride will not last forever but will in fact come to an end. Between these two limits is the span and experience of an earthly life.

For practical reasons, during their lives most people give up some power. Unfortunately, most people never manage the power dynamic very well. As we have discussed previously, each individual has a governing element. Often, the struggle for control of what we call "me," "self," or "I" is between the ego (that component of self grounded in the physical world) and a higher self (that aspect of being aligned with divine intelligence).

This struggle for control (the fight between ego and the higher self) is, for many people, the defining feature of life. When ego gains the upper hand, life is a competition to survive. When the higher self gains control, life becomes a cooperative adventure, a playful quest, a joyous ride. The analogy offered here is to get you to consider, for all the choices you make, for the intentions you have, the desires you nurture, and the feelings you feel - something bigger than the "you" on the ride, controls the ride.

The controller always acts in your best interest. The power of the individual comes from a greater source.

You are not separate from that power, but to experience the thrill of the ride, you detach from the controls. You must let go. As it is with each individually, it is with the whole. The "system" - the ride - is a function of the whole. We, you and I, are experiencing elements of the whole. The whole is controlled by an aspect of you bigger than you, greater than you. The grand design, the majestic epic, the creative story - this ride - is bigger than any individual. You are one with the whole, and in this life contribute to the whole. Fulfill your role. Ride your ride. Leave the controls to the controller - everything will be okay.

Now, the ride is in good hands - the big picture is secure. Your little piece of reality however, is not quite as defined. While the end game is assured; the details are up to you. The decisions you make and the circumstances you create determine where the ride takes you. The ride is designed to allow extreme creativity and simultaneously is a vehicle that produces maximum impact. The ride can generate thrills or spills, delightful twists or gut-wrenching turns. The ride can fly free and fast, or stall and dive low and slow. The choices you make determine where the ride goes and what you experience along the way.

Always remember something else: divine intelligence maintains a vigilant watch and retains ultimate control. All for your greater good. Part of the challenge of the journey of life is learning or knowing whom to trust on the ride and with whom to share power. You are on the ride of your life. You have chosen to ride. You steer the ride. You interpret the sensations the ride generates. Another aspect of yourself - divine intelligence - controls the ride. Ultimately your trust must be in divine intelligence. Otherwise your entire life is a struggle. Fear will cause you to resist. If you don't trust the ride will hold together, or you don't trust that divine intelligence will operate the ride safely - for your benefit - your experience on the ride is going to suffer. You are going to suffer.

Trust in both the integrity of the ride and the reliability of the controller.

Reflecting on the motives of the individual, ask yourself: What moves you? Where do you steer the ride and why? Most people offer a multitude of answers to this query. Some think the course of the ride is fixed (fate). Some think the course of the ride depends on luck (chance). Some believe other people steer the ride, or the environment or circumstances set the course. These people contend the ride is an experience they endure - not an adventure they select. For people who think this way - that they have no say in what the ride brings - sometimes the ride is under control; sometimes it is not. Sometimes, as riders, they get to enjoy the thrill; sometimes they just must endure.

The reality is, the choices you make determine both the nature of the circumstances you encounter and how you interpret the experience. Don't let the ego steer your ride. If you want to get the most out of the ride, work with the controller. Work with, not against, divine intelligence.

Go where the ride leads you, willingly and enthusiastically. On the ride of your life - trust that the thrills and spills, the twists and the turns, the bumps and the rolls - are for a purpose; are for your highest good. But remember, as you steer, you can modify the course of the ride. Reinforce the good, temper the bad - get the most thrills out of the journey. Divine intelligence controls the ride. Work together with divine intelligence, trust in divine intelligence, and you can't go wrong.

LIVE LIFE TO THE FULLEST

Life is to experience, distinct and apart from the whole. You have a mission: to be a light in the darkness, a cheerleader, a champion. Your mission is to engage in the fray, offer a hand, offer a smile - to always point the way. By living life to the fullest you bless everyone.

A guiding light of truth beckons. Your destiny awaits. Move toward and embrace truth or endure the trials of life idling on the sideline. In living your life, you cannot be for or against truth. You are either for truth or not. Like electricity fills a line, current either flows or is not present - there is no state of "off." In your life, you either act to fulfill your purpose or you do not. You cannot be against truth, but in an illusion. Find your way out of the illusion.

"I am the way, the truth and the life..." Do you get it or did you miss it?

These words of Jesus aren't referring to the physical body or even to a historical figure. The truth and wisdom of His claim are as valid and timeless now as when spoken two thousand years ago.

The way, truth, and life are a realization.

You are connected to all people, to all creatures, to all things, timeless, immortal and complete. This is the reality Jesus professed. You are not lost and alone. Recognize and embrace the spirit of truth to awaken to a new life, to rise anew; to live a full life.

Jesus proclaimed, as do all enlightened teachers, that you are of one, in all, of all.

You are not entombed in time or space but can in fact transcend the boundaries you cling to so adamantly in this life. By transcending, the teacher pointed the way. Through the still, small voice of truth you are called home. Infinite love and compassion embraces those who believe they are not whole, but are rather lost in the illusion of their choice. Truth calls out, lights a flame, waits patiently, joyfully and without fail. The only responsibility you bear, you asked for, is to make the choice.

In the end, "The right will be done." There is no other will - stop resisting.

The way and the reality of bliss are with and in you, here and now, in this instant, regardless of what manifests in experience. Your life can change in an instant - this instant, if you awaken to the spirit that is love, that is now. The choice, by grace, is yours to make. Grasp the wisdom to see, hear, and understand.

Embrace the truth, for the truth will set you free. You will then experience life to its fullest.

ACT DESPITE FEAR

Fear, the primordial instinct that serves to keep us alive in a sometimes dangerous world, is corrupted by ego and used against us. Most people are lost in ego, in the power struggle of survival and control. Ego seeks to dominate. Blind to ego's intentions, we seek comfort and solace in what we know. Enmeshed in ego we learn to avoid fear rather than face it, and in so doing tie our own hands, bind our thinking, limit our possibilities. To succeed in this life, come to terms with fear and move beyond it. To secure the knowledge that you are enduring, that you exist beyond your immediate circumstances, whole, safe and secure - act despite fear.

Fear is from ego. Fear is energy generated from within. Fear paralyzes and inhibits action. Courage is the capacity to face fear; to face what is imagined. Courage is the ability to generate positive energy to overcome fear. Only by truly being at peace in this world can you eliminate fear from your experience. In the meantime, to move in the direction of promise and possibility you must act despite fear. You must face fear - not to combat it, but rather to recognize it when and where it exists.

In crisis situations some people are able to act quickly and decisively, not allowing fear to muffle a response. Positive motives overcome fear. However, in everyday circumstances where people have the luxury of time and distance, they often allow the seed of fear to grow. You nurture fear with your intellect and your imagination. In these circumstances, only by facing fear, only by stepping outside its influence through awareness, are you able to expose fear for the deception it is.

For those lost in the illusion - clinging tightly to the substance of this life, strength of desire is the lever to overcome fear. Do you want it badly enough, whatever "it" may be?

Fear is energy intent on slowing life down. Fears binds you, restrains you, limits you. Instead of succumbing to fear's embrace, recognize and release it. Don't resist fear, rather work with it, reshape it, redirect it. Change fear to exhilaration, to anticipation, to excitement, by breathing into it. Add the energy of your body to the apprehension of fear. As you breathe deeper and fuller (literally - from your diaphragm), excite the fear, expand it, change it.

By facing fear and acting you conquer fear. Recognize fear for what it is, energy applied by ego to keep you submissive to ego's will. By recognizing, observing and reshaping fear you dissolve it. Once you free yourself from the grip of fear you can move forward. The more you exercise your essence, your awareness, the more you limit fear's hold. Make a habit of acting despite fear. Deliberately change fear to exuberance. As you install new habits of dealing with fear, you will arrive at a state of being where fear has no influence.

Action fuels courage. Courage leads to wisdom and wisdom to fulfillment. Act despite fear and live a fulfilling life.

A DECISION, A CHOICE MAKES THE DIFFERENCE - THAT CHOICE IS YOURS

In all of human history, human nature has not changed, nor have the rules of the game.

Something greater than you, but something you have access to and are part of, is writing the story - the drama, the adventure, the comedy, the romance. You are creation and creator. You have a part to play, a very specific part, in the sweeping revelation of history. You possess the ultimate power - you can choose.

The only difference between the super successful, the wealthy, the powerful leaders, the insightful contributors, the innovators, the adventures and you is a decision.

You choose the direction and the speed of your life. Your potential is unlimited.

Moving in some direction is a given - it is a law, a requirement of life. The key, the wisdom, the secret is in that choice. You get to choose the direction.

Are you going to wallow in indecision, letting the prevailing winds, the current, or the ride carry you where they may? Or are you going to chart your course, set your sails, create the adventure and advance on a course of your choosing? Your choice is the difference. Your choice is the next step.

TAKE THE NEXT STEP

Life sometimes seems like a daunting challenge. The span, the tasks, the competition, the limitations all converge in the lonely, and often seemingly isolated intellect to squelch motivation and restrict potential.

When all seems too much and you believe you are going through hell, the thing to do is to keep going. Only by moving forward will you progress beyond the circumstances that hold you back.

Countless lives have been wasted clinging needlessly and hopelessly to a mirage of how life was. When time seems to stand still, and not in a good way; when hope seems lost, it is time to call up the courage to advance, to take a step forward. When it seems darkest, take a step into the light, take the next step.

If you have lost your way and life seems overwhelming, recognize this truth: you never take on the entire experience of life at once. All that stuff, all those demands and all those expectations are burdens or blessings of your choosing. Raise your sights, look up - the weight of the world only rests on you in your imagination. You assume those burdens then bear them endlessly because of fear - fear of change - worry for what the future might hold. In truth, you never reach the breadth and depth, urgency and fury of the future; you only journey there in your thoughts.

The challenge of life is manageable, but only if you keep going. Life is a journey - trek on.

The events of life, the small slice of time, space and circumstances marking existence are, by design, narrow. Intentions bring the circumstances you face and the conditions you either enjoy or endure. Intend to explore anew. As a human being you have a natural capacity to absorb and interpret. Don't limit the opportunity by stifling the motion. When you stop, life stops. When you are overcome by fear, your capacity to create is lost. Don't let fear cloud your awareness with unnecessary self-imposed restrictions. Move forward in a positive direction. Keep life and the events of living in perspective.

Courage allows you to move forward, to achieve the promise and potential that is your gift - your birthright. This life requires you do only one thing - take one small step - then do it over again.

Nothing beyond that matters. To live a full and fulfilling life, to make the journey of life worthwhile, take the most important step of your life - take the next step. Life works when you do.

ONE FINAL TIME

We are closing in on the finish. You are almost at the end of this volume.

If you have reached the end, by way of the middle, you've been given several important themes, stated in diverse ways. Repetition here substitutes for power. So in the interest of trying to internalize these ideas, I'll leave you to ponder these important truths:

You determine your reality.
Though it appears life is happening to you, life is happening for you. Life is about feeling, and you have a variety of options to choose from. If you choose and reinforce good feelings, you receive and get to experience more good feelings. Love is the ultimate good feeling. If you choose anything less, you get something less. You get what you give. Life responds to you.

An accurate measure of achievement is not what one gets, but rather what one gives. Changing the world "out there" begins by changing the world "in here." Give love, grow love, become love. There is no higher calling.

Here is The Success Spectrum one final time. The surrounding oval is meant to portray context. Your individual life happens within a larger context - a larger reality of truth, and faith, and love. You choose where along the action continuum you live your life. You decide how fast you move, how hard you accelerate. You choose your perspective. The grand bargain is, however, that you only see life from the position, the perspective, you choose. Your view is limited by the place you claim. Every place has value. And while some are better than others every position is secure.

Ultimately life will prevail. Your existence is a component of a broader whole. Your welfare is assured, but the choice - your place in time and space - is your decision. You reinforce your decision, you plot your course, with every thought you entertain and every feeling you release into the world. You are master of your fate.

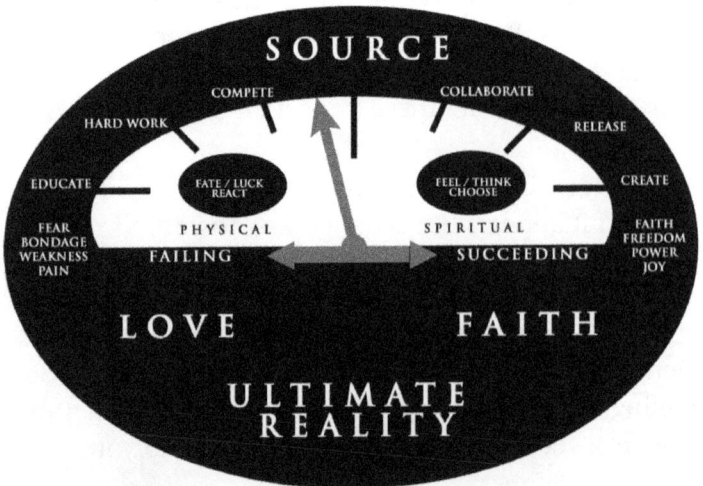

SOURCE

COMPETE   COLLABORATE

HARD WORK   RELEASE

EDUCATE   FATE / LUCK   FEEL / THINK   CREATE
             REACT   CHOOSE

FEAR   FAITH
BONDAGE   PHYSICAL   SPIRITUAL   FREEDOM
WEAKNESS   FAILING   SUCCEEDING   POWER
PAIN   JOY

LOVE   FAITH

ULTIMATE
REALITY

THE SUCCUSS SPECTRUM IN CONTEXT

Move up the scale. Move in the right direction. Choose a broader perspective. See farther and wider - a world of infinite possibility exists. You need only believe to make the impossible possible. No matter where you are, or where you choose to be, never despair - life is designed for your wellbeing. Everything is under control. Remember, you are one with the whole.

You are responsible.
Life is your opportunity, your task, your mission. It is your choice. While the source - divine will, infinite intelligence - is in charge, you are responsible. You are part of the divine whole. You are not separate from God. Your will is divine will. Don't let ego steal your life. Don't let negativity shackle you to mediocrity. Live life to the full. Make divine will your will - follow where divine will guides you.

Within you is the still, small voice - your true, eternal self - calling out, "I am here. I am the source of all you need." Listen.

Move in the right direction.
Life is motion - you will only get where you intend to go by deliberately steering that way. Everyone is meant to succeed. The circumstances of life are not what matters - only your responses do, and every response is a choice. By making the right choices you move in the right direction.

Choose well - ask - then let go. Each thought is a new choice.

If you still feel desire, you have growing to do - life to live - keep moving.

Life is an outdoor sport and not a spectator sport. Get out there. Get in the game and enjoy.

As Henry David Thoreau expressed:

> ***Advance confidently in the direction of your dreams and endeavor to live the life you imagine, and you will meet with success unexpected in common hours.***

Life works when you do. Get to work on yourself. You have infinite potential in a world of endless possibility - get going. Know the rules of life. Play by the rules and win.

We're all here with you!

Success 101: How Life Works

AFTERWORD

We have journeyed a long way together. We have discovered the "secrets" aren't really secrets after all. They are rather truths most deny as unbelievable or that most fear to accept.

Life is all about experience - energy and awareness performing an intricate dance. Each life is an opportunity to participate in and contribute to that dance. Each life is an opportunity to experience and to create. Everything is in motion, and so are we. We get to feel, to think, and to move, and then to feel some more. Success is ultimately a feeling - a good feeling. While we operate as if we are independent entities, the reality is we are dependent parts of an integrated whole. We have desires, we make choices, we move. We create experience with the powerful creative energy of thought. We realize enduring good feelings - feelings of success - when we move in concert with life; when we move in the right direction. It's all so simple.

Each individual is both ultimately powerful and ultimately responsible; a very scary proposition. The single obstacle to overwhelming success is the force of ego - that component of self that insists on standing apart. Life operates by law. The three most significant of which are: 1. Life intends to grow; 2. Thoughts become things; and 3. One receives in proportion to what one gives.

The single most important thing is focus (the goal or objective) because that focus determines direction of travel. The route from fear to faith is traversed by taking small, measured steps in the right direction. One must both choose and act - this is what it means to live.

Each individual is part of the collective. Each person contributes a portion of his or her power usually intentionally, but sometimes unwittingly to the functioning of society. The political and economic systems we enjoy or endure are a function of that collective contribution. Each of us is responsible for what we collectively get.

To take control of your life. You must assume complete and total responsibility for yourself - the good and the bad. Then you have to make the biggest leap of all. You have to have faith - let go, stop resisting - choose wisely and act. Feelings will guide you. The still, small voice within is a constant, trustworthy companion. Acting for the right reasons, the right motives, will surely bring you the full and fulfilling life you deserve.

Thank you for taking this journey with me. You see, the energy you devote to seeking the truth brightens and empowers that path making it more accessible to everyone.

Receive now what you have found. Believe what you receive. Become what you believe.

All the best as you continue your journey. Remember, by *playing* you win and we win!

Till we meet again (and rest assured we shall),

Scott F. Paradis

ACKNOWLEDGEMENTS

Everything I have done, everything I do, and everything I am yet to do is made possible by the loving and supportive people that surround me and by those that are drawn into my awareness. It is their genius and their generosity that make my accomplishments possible.

For Lisa, my wife, and my two terrific children, Merideth and Mitchell, I am forever grateful. I am truly blessed having them in my life.

To my mother Muriel, for a lifetime of sacrifice and prayers on my behalf, and for the enthusiastic encouragement of my sister Renee; to my father Arthur, my sister Luree, and my extended family and friends I owe endless thanks. By the examples of those closest to me, courageously questioning, diligently searching, and faithfully acting, I have come to realize an authentic revelation: life is a collective journey for our common good.

Success 101 How Life Works is not a singular achievement. The ideas from this book fill the gap of time and space from antiquity to modernity. The ideas relayed in this work are the wisdom and insights of countless people; from authors whose names have been lost to the annals of history to contemporary theorists and practitioners who render plain nearly unfathomable truths. To ancient writers and modern day prophets expressing ultimate reality through inspiring words, I extend my deepest thanks.

The lights that others shine guide me on my journey. My prayer is that I might also cast some light to help others find their way. Together we fill the adventure with joy and love.

Success 101: How Life Works

ABOUT THE AUTHOR

Scott F. Paradis is a student of life and a seeker of ultimate truth. A native of New Hampshire, he has spent the last three decades traveling the world working national security issues, observing the remarkable similarities of people from diverse cultures, and pondering "weighty" questions: Why are we here? and Where are we headed?

Scott retired as a colonel at the end of 2011 after serving more than 30 years with the United States Army. He served in the Middle East, Europe, and at various stations in the United States. His military and civilian education includes Senior Service College, a national security fellowship at Harvard University; a Congressional fellowship with the United States Senate; a masters degree from Central Michigan University; a bachelors degree from the University of New Hampshire; and assorted professional and skill specific training. His military awards and decorations range from the Legion of Merit and Bronze Star, to multiple service, commendation, and achievement medals and ribbons.

Scott lives with his beautiful wife of 26 years, Lisa, in Alexandria, Virginia. Together they have two terrific children - Merideth and Mitchell.

Contact Scott at the Success 101 Workshop (Success-101Workshop.com) now to help you and your organization move in a worthwhile, productive, and prosperous direction. Choose to improve your business and your life.

Success 101: How Life Works

SUCCESS101WORKSHOP.COM

The *Success 101 Workshop* helps individuals and teams succeed in business and life. Through insightful messages, hands-on workshops, and focused courses and presentations *Success 101 Workshop* helps businesses prosper and people live full and fulfilling lives. *Success 101 Workshop* programs help people uncover their foremost desires, develop their innate talents, and leverage their personal power to create and live the lives of their dreams.

Scott F. Paradis, founder and principle trainer of the *Success 101 Workshop*, trains individuals and teams to excel.

Success in business and in life is not a matter of employing overwhelming resources and commanding irresistible power, it is a matter of doing the best you can with what you've got. By learning and leveraging the fundamental principles of leadership and success you can change your mind, your business, and your life.

Through hands-on workshops and focused presentations, *Success 101 Workshop* broadens people's perspectives so they see with greater clarity and come to understand what is most important. Armed with that knowledge they can act with greater confidence to succeed and prosper.

About Success 101 Workshop

Books:

Success 101 How Life Works
Know the Rules, Play to Win
Scott F. Paradis, Cornerstone Achievements, 2012

E-book (.PDF) with Volume 2, *Words and Deeds*, and audio and audio-visual bonus materials at Success101Workshop. com

Hard Cover, Soft Cover, E-Readers - available where books are sold

Warrior, Diplomats, Heroes:
Why America's Army Succeeds
Lessons for Business and Life
Scott F. Paradis, Cornerstone Achievements, 2012

E-book (.PDF) with audio, and audio-visual bonus materials at Success101Workshop.com

Hard Cover, Soft Cover, E-Readers - available where books are sold

Promise and Potential
A Life of Wisdom, Courage, Strength and Will
Scott F. Paradis, Cornerstone Achievements, 2008

E-book with bonus material and Hard Cover - at Success-101Workshop.com

Self-Study Courses:

Success 101 How Life Works

Warriors, Diplomats, Heroes - Leading from the Front

NOTES

NOTES

www.ingramcontent.com/pod-product-compliance
Lightning Source LLC
Chambersburg PA
CBHW022015090426
42739CB00006BA/146